CITY BOY

Joseph Jurlina

CITY BOY

Published by *KC* Paper Company

©2013 Joseph Jurlina
ISBN: 978-0-615-70517-0
Biography/Memoir/Genealogy

ALL RIGHTS RESERVED

Manufacturing by Lulu.com
Cover Design by Katherine A. Clark
Photo Credit Ralph Perkin

KC Paper Co.
2522 State Route 208
Walden, NY 12586
KCPaperCompany.com

Printed in the United States of America

CITY BOY

By Joseph Jurlina

TABLE OF CONTENTS

Autobiography 9

Appendix A: Photographs 187

Appendix B: Documents 260

Appendix C: Trip Diaries 273

Appendix D: Pedigree Chart.................... 293

Joseph Jurlina

ACKNOWLEDGEMENTS

This bit of history was possible only because of the encouragement of my wife Billie John Grable Jurlina, *Country Girl*, and the effort of our granddaughter, Katherine Allison Krumm Clark, who has the ability to get a job done. I would also like to thank Mike and Carol Ann for the efforts and hours of sorting through and gathering the appropriate photographs and documents and Bill for using his computer savvy scanning them all and sending them to be included in the book.

Katherine Clark would like to thank her grandfather for taking the time to document his life and memories. She is grateful for the opportunity, joy, and privilege of getting to know her grandfather so much better through working on this project! She also hopes that it will help someone to connect with and learn more about their heritage and the generations who have gone before.

DISCLAIMER

The information provided here is accurate and true to the best of our knowledge. It is possible that unintentional mistakes and oversights have been made as well as omissions. We apologize in advance for such occurrences and hope that this missive will be useful for the informative purposes for which it was intended.

CITY BOY

JOSEPH JURLINA

CITY BOY

AN AUTOBIOGRAPHY

An autobiography is not the easiest thing to write, especially for me, because throughout my life I have had more interest in other people than in myself. That is probably a reflection of my early environment in which you were to mind your own business and you were supposed to learn more by listening than talking. Further, everyone I knew felt that 'the other fellows' were smarter and had more positive attributes than you did - but more about that later.

The bulk of this autobiography is in response to questions posed in a DOS computer program which I was given by someone. It deals with all aspects of life and is not necessarily in chronological order; therefore, the jumping back and forth from one subject to another makes it difficult for me to be consistent in my responses and probably there will be repetitions.

You may wonder why a grown man would even try to write his life story. In my case, this is the third effort. First, as a senior in high school I was given an opportunity to write an autobiography of two thousand words or less just to demonstrate that our schooling had not been a complete waste of time. Second, a year or so after my retirement in 1987, I decided that I should leave at least some notes about my life, as uninteresting as

CITY BOY

that might be to my progeny, just to answer the why, where, or when questions asked about parents. This third attempt is to clarify the first two in the hope that I will have left more information and history about me and my ancestors than were left for us. You the reader will have to be the judge as to whether I accomplished what I set out to do.

ORIGINS AND NAMES

JOSEPH JURLINA AT ABOUT AGE THREE IN 1927

Joseph Jurlina, the subject of this dissertation, was born on Monday, 19 September 1924, at home located at 1157 East 63rd Street in Cleveland, Cuyahoga County, Ohio. I was delivered with the assistance of a mid-wife named Marijana Puc who lived just up the street and around the corner on 64th Street, a total of about 300 yards from my parent's home. Marijana delivered the first four children in our family. Mary Jane, the youngest, was the only one delivered by a medical doctor, Dr. Oman, in a hospital. Doctor Oman was our family doctor for many years.

According to those present at my birth, I weighed in at nine pounds but no report about length was ever disclosed to me. What hair I had was very blonde and stayed blonde most of my life through about 21 years. My face was on the round side and my eyes were green. As I remember, most people remarked how I looked more like my mother and her family than my father. No birthmarks were reported. If my memory is accurate I started walking at about 9-10 months not having crawled much before.

My hair stayed blonde throughout the time I was exposed to the sun for a few hours each day. As I aged my hair turned a bit darker like my mother's hair and, as in the case of my mother who had few gray hair when she died eleven days before her 56th birthday, my hair started graying only after I was in my sixties. I was average in height for most of my pre-teen years but grew rather quickly after I got into high school and I grew about six inches while in high school ending up at 74 inches. Most of my years before age fifty I weighed in at 185 to 195, except while in the service. I weighed 205 when I was discharged.

My parents, Thomas Jurlina and Mary Telban Jurlina, named me Joseph supposedly for my paternal grandfather whom I never met because he lived in Seline, Velebit, Croatia. Croatia was a part of Jugoslavia during WWII but since 1991 has been restored as the independent Republic of Croatia. I was not given a middle name for a reason unknown to me. My brother Edward, who died at about nine months of age, also was not given a middle name. All my other siblings were given middle names - Thomas John, Robert Stephen and Mary Jane. I must assume that the middle name John given to my brother Tommy was taken from my maternal grandfather John J. Telban. That was never discussed in our family that I can recall.

Through most of my childhood mother called me Joey and my father called me Joso (pronounced Yosho) while my contemporaries called me Joe or Joe Buckeye, often shortened to Buckeye. The Joe Buckeye came from Tony Vidmar, brother of my best friend and schoolmate Albert James Anthony Vidmar. Strangers to our ethnic neighborhood often used the less endearing name 'Hey Hunkie' which did not refer to my stature but rather to the assumed central European origin of my parents. The use of the term 'Hunkie' in reference to me or many of my contemporaries always complicated our lives and those who used the term. To say that we had many fist fights as children minimizes the story. My father was born in Seline, Croatia. He often talked about his early life in Seline where he spent much of his first seventeen years harvesting wood for the cooking and heating of their rather modest stone home. My mother was born in Cleveland, Ohio, of parents born in Slovenia.

It was not until after I retired and acquired a Personal Computer equipped with word-processing software that I felt compelled to make some notes about our family roots. I was especially concerned that our children had not heard all the details of Billie's and my early time together and how this family of Jurlinas came to be located in Richardson, Texas. Specific details about individuals and families in our clan are detailed in the data files of a genealogical data package called Personal Ancestral File (PAF) collected primarily by myself with the help of my wife Billie, Billie's cousin Kathryn Brown Howell, and my cousin William George Avenmarg, and all the other members of our family. The data files or printouts of all family data are included at least partially in the appendix of this report.

ANCESTRY OF THE JURLINA CLAN

In the past two to three years much of the Jurlina ancestral data was given to me by Sime Jurlina (Sam or Simeon), who in May 1995 moved from the port city of Tivat, Montenegro to the Island of Brac, Croatia, located about 10-15 miles off the South Coast of Split, Croatia. Because of the civil war in former Jugoslavia (started about 1990) the former states of Jugoslavia, Slovenia and Croatia particularly, treat all new immigrants from Jugoslavia as refugees. Sime is classified as a refugee on the Island of Brac from Montenegro, and as such, he and his wife Nevenka could not seek permanent employment in Croatia until their status is changed. A process he believed would take a year. I have not heard about any change.

My cousin, Ante Jurlina, son of my father's youngest sister (Antica), has provided some information about his family. At that time he lived in the port city of Zadar with his wife. Zadar is located about 40 miles southeast of Seline, the birthplace of my father and Ante. The data provided by Ante and Sime included names of people with a few locations but very little with respect to dates and details of children in various families.

Vesna Jurlina Hrestak, a cousin who lives in Sassolburg, South Africa, has given me some information about her family. She is the daughter of my first cousin Rudolph Jurlina who lived in Zagreb, the capitol of the Republic of Croatia. He was born in 1921 and died in 2004.

Members of the Jurlina clan live in many parts of the world and some of them have provided data for their immediate families: Mate Jurlina presently lives in Imperial Beach (Cathedral City), California; Milan Jurlina lives in Vancouver, British Columbia, Canada; Joseph Jurlina lives in Columbus, Ohio; Peter Jurlina who lived in Lowellville, Ohio died about 2000. John, son of Peter lived in Florida. At least three families of Jurlinas live in Australia but have not answered my letters of inquiry about their family origin nor provided any data. Two families on the North Island of New Zealand have given me much data about their families but we have not been able to tie them directly to our line. A Damir Jurlina in Long Island, New York has communicated some data to us also but his line started in Zadar and I have not been able to tie his line into ours as yet. There is a family in New Jersey but they do not respond to letters. Ljubica Zuze Jurac, a descendant of my Uncle Sam Jurlina, lives in Mamaroneck, New York and has sent some data on her family. Ljubica has Jurlina ancestors on both sides of her family. The most significant contribution to our data base of Jurlinas has come from Tomo Jurlina who has lived in Belgrade, Serbia most of his life. Tomo was born in 1928, and is the son of Sime, my father's younger brother. A Family Tree of the JURLINA clan as described by data in my PAF database and another produced by a software package called Family Tree Maker (FTM) is on my desk in a rolled up form of one kind or another. This product may be somewhat dated but was the best available at the time.

Although many names in the Jurlina family tree are based on data given by Sime Jurlina, of the Island of Brac, Croatia, Tome Jurlina of Belgrade, Serbia has given me much data recently and in July 2007 he mailed a report on the Jurlina Family of Seline, Croatia – it appears to be a wonderfully complete summary of the Jurlinas of the Seline area but it is written in Serbo-Croatian, a language of which I know very little. Perhaps at some future date we can get it translated. Copies of that report are also in my desk.

Not much is known of my ancestors in Croatia or Slovenia. Some pictures are available and are kept in my filing cabinet and on the bookcase of my

CITY BOY

office. Some are held by Michael and Carol Ann, but as I mentioned previously not much in the way of photographs is available. Many family photos are in my correspondence files in loose-leaf binders in my office. These were prepared for our 60th wedding anniversary celebration.

As you might have already guessed, my father spoke Serbo-Croatian while my mother grew up in a family that spoke English and Slovenian. Mom and Dad communicated with each other in English under normal circumstances but when the children were present, they spoke their 'mother tongues' so that we could not understand the gist of the conversation. In addition, World War I had just come to an end in 1917 just seven years before I was born when the anti-German sentiment was still very high; therefore, English was the preferred language and our parents were adamant about speaking English at all times. As a result, my siblings and I grew up without any training in the other languages available. At this time we believe we were deprived of an opportunity to be bi-lingual.

MY TELBAN GRANDPARENTS

Mary Novak/Telban/Jeric/Virant
BORN 25 JANUARY 1882 — DIED 28 OCTOBER 1948

Grandfather John Telban, my mother's father, was murdered in 1917 in his saloon, seven years before my birth, so I unfortunately never knew him. All our exposure to grandparents was with our maternal grandmother "Gramma" Novak Telban who lived just a few blocks from our home on East 63rd Street. Gramma was available to us but she spoke little English having lived in an ethnic community from the time of her arrival in the USA about 1902. In spite of the language barrier she and I communicated with each other

Joseph Jurlina

Dec. 17/917

MASKED GUNMEN KILL TWO IN CAFE

Proprietor and Customer Shot Down Without Word From Bandits.

Revenge Believed Motive of Slayers, Who Make Escape.

Walking into the saloon of John Telban, 900 E. 61st street, at 10:40 last night two masked men shot and killed Frank Juh, 20, a customer, 1002 E. 61st street, then turned their guns on Telban and shot him dead. Telban was shot five times and Juh twice.

Three employees of the East Ohio Gas Co. were sitting at a table in the front of the bar room. The masked men turned their revolvers on them and told them to keep quiet, then backed out of the front door. No attempt was made to rifle the cash register.

Telban's wife, five daughters and a son were asleep in their rooms above the saloon, but were awakened by the shots and came running down the stairs.

Police were notified and Patrolman Frank Wilcox was first to arrive, followed by Detectives Somers, Page, Sager, Smetana, Sergt. Promer, Capt. May, Capt. Farr and Assistant Chief of Detectives Thomas Mahoney.

Fire at Juh First.

The gas employes said no words passed between the men when they entered. They pointed their revolvers and two shots were immediately fired at Juh. When he fell, they say Telban reached under the bar for a heavy beer glass and the men opened fire on him as he threw it at one of the gunmen.

Explaining the fact that there was no attempt at robbery, police early this morning said that for some time there has been a series of holdups on E. 61st street and that Telban had been giving police valuable information regarding suspicious persons that had come into the saloon.

He also was one of the principal witnesses recently against several men who staged a holdup a short distance from the saloon. Shortly before the cases came up friends of the prisoners tried to prevail upon Telban to keep secret.

This leads the detectives to believe that the shooting was done in a spirit of revenge.

The East Ohio company's employes were taken to Central station in an effort to have them identify pictures in the Rogues' gallery. They gave their names as John Flora, George Katz and John Urie.

Juh was about to be called to the National army.

The bodies of the victims were taken to the county morgue.

These two articles documented the murder of John Telban in his saloon and are from the Cleveland Plain Dealer and the The Cleveland Press from December 1917.

rather well I thought. I am not certain whether she or I gained more from our association.

We dearly loved Gramma because she dearly loved us and displayed that love more than anyone else in the family. My favorite memory about my Gramma would have to be going to her home and helping her bake and eat Potica, her home-baked pies of all kinds, and better still her home-made rye bread in the round.

Gramma remarried within a year after her first husband was killed. Frank Jeric was her second husband, a marriage that lasted about nineteen years before they divorced because of his excessive drinking of alcohol. The grandchildren liked Frank very much but we were distanced from him by his drinking. My Aunt Julia was their only child.

Florian Virant, Gramma's third husband, was a tailor of sorts but by reputation a better drinker than a tailor. None of the adults in our family of relatives were fond of his presence. He was a typical European male who tried to dominate his wife like and as a result was practically ignored by all except my mother and father. My parents felt a responsibility to protect Gramma as best they could by visiting often enough to be aware of the relationship with Florian.

Gramma died in 1948 and Florian died in 1954 - from 1948 until 1954 Florian must have lived a lonely life because he was ignored like the plague. Between her divorce from Frank and shortly after her marriage to Florian, Frank Jeric stopped his drinking, probably because of his health, and became a very reasonable sort of guy. My father said on many occasions that had he done that earlier Gramma would not have had any cause to divorce him.

Our family had a strong sense of its ethnic background as evidenced in the foods we ate and the way weddings, baptisms and other holidays were celebrated. The music of the ethnic community was clearly central European in nature with polkas and fast waltzes the popular choices. Frank Yankovich was a local musical hero who rose to national prominence in the polka band world. He died in 1998 at the age of 83. Data available on the Internet spells his name Jankovich which would

Joseph Jurlina

indicate to me he was of Croatia or Serbian descent. Our dress was only unique in the sense it was 'depression dress' precipitated by the economic hardship of the times.

ORIGIN OF GRANDPARENTS AND THEIR EDUCATION

As I mentioned previously, my mother's parents, John J. Telban and Mary Novak Telban, came to the USA about 1902 and settled in Cleveland, Cuyahoga County, Ohio immediately. It is my uncertain understanding that they were married after they arrived in the States. Grandmother came from Novo Mesto, Slovenia, which is about half way between Ljubljana (capitol of Slovenia) and Zagreb, or about 50 miles East of Ljubljana. My grandfather Telban apparently came from a small community of Borovnica about 10 miles Southwest of Ljubljana also in Slovenia. There is a community of the same spelling not too far from Novo Mesto and it may well be that he was born there. I am sure that they both left their homeland to come to the USA, the land of economic opportunity, to make their fortune and then return to their homeland; however, neither ever returned to their place of birth. I feel almost certain that they settled in Cleveland because of the friendly ethnic environment that existed so they could continue speaking their native tongue. They also must have had some communication from other friends who had come to Cleveland earlier.

My grandparents born in Slovenia and Croatia had very little education and I expect that they did not get beyond the equivalent of elementary school. My mother completed elementary school in Cleveland and then attended business school. Many of the children of these ancestors attended college and became professionals in various fields. Those that grew up during the depression often realized the importance of education and pursued their studies diligently.

Most of my ancestors were Roman Catholics but it may be that some in Croatia were Greek Orthodox. Most of the family members in the USA are nominal Roman Catholics as was I, until I left home for service in the Army of the USA in 1943. Following marriage to Billie J. Grable, she and I attended the Methodist Church in which Billie had grown up. We attended the Methodist Church as a family until 1959 when we were admitted in the Episcopal Church USA. There should be more about that subject later in this epistle.

Based on present knowledge most of our ancestors in Croatia and Slovenia were involved in agricultural pursuits. My father and most of my American relatives were involved in various common labor jobs although they all were very proficient in their chosen careers and were long-term employees with the companies with whom they were employed. Most of our ancestral families had 4-6 children and I would guess was typical of agricultural family units. Most of the families were relatively low-income families and did not have many assets to pass down to their children. Land holdings in Croatia and Slovenia were, by government edict, confined to small plots, and plots that were not contiguous or adjacent to other holdings. That is, if the family accumulated 5-10 acres the land might contain 10-20 small lots scattered over the countryside.

JOSEPH JURLINA, BORN 2 JANUARY 1859, DIED 26 JULY 1939
FATHER OF THOMAS JURLINA, BORN 31 MAY 1896, DIED 22 OCTOBER 1979
GRANDFATHER OF JOSEPH, EDWARD, THOMAS J., ROBERT S. & MARY JANE

JOSEPH JURLINA IN SELINE, CROATIA – ABT 1938
FATHER OF THOMAS JURLINA

2 JANUARY 1859   26 JULY 1939

My ancestors on my father's side lived to enjoy ages from 80-90 years but I have no knowledge whether there were any common illnesses that caused their deaths. On the other hand, my mother's parents and ancestors managed to live 60-75 with some few exceptions. My grandmother Telban's youngest brother Joseph died at age 93 in the USA.

My grandmother Telban died from complications of sugar diabetes in 1948. My mother died of lung cancer at the age of 56 in 1960 while my father died at age 83 of unknown causes in 1979.

OUR FAMILY HEIRLOOMS

There are not any significant heirlooms in our family although our daughter Carol Ann has two pieces of furniture that my parents purchased in 1922, the year they married. My parents were fairly typical of the people born about 1900 in central Europe and in ethnic neighborhoods. My father was a strong-willed rather shy person who had stronger convictions about fair play and being faithful to friends as long as they lived up to his expectations of them. Any breach of this friendship resulted in a total breaking-off of the relationship. As a young man he had black hair and never to my knowledge weighed more than 170 pounds although he was about 74 inches tall. Mother was a brown-haired person about 65 inches tall and never exceeded 120 pounds until very late in life. She, too, was a shy person. I always attributed that to her background in an ethnic family growing up in and having children during a severe economic depression. Mom's short exposure to the business world as a secretary, left her with the feeling that her generation would always work for others most of their lives. She could not imagine anyone not being truthful in all dealings with other people. Her sense of fairness was stronger than my fathers but with much less noise.

MY FATHER THOMAS JURLINA BORN IN SELINE, CROATIA

Father arrived in New York City and docked at Ellis Island for processing aboard the steamship Martha Washington on 25 October 1913 at the age of seventeen. Apparently the trip took almost eleven days during which my father spent much time "at the railing". His father and his uncles had purchased a one-way steerage-ticket and he departed from the port of Split, Croatia. Family lore has it that my father's parents and cousins fully expected a war to break out in Europe, and, having lost other members of the family in wars, they wanted him kept safe. As it turned out World War I did start after the assassination of Franz Josef in 1914. My father had hoped to return to Croatia at some future date, but as it was he died at age 83 without having ever returned to Seline, Croatia even for a visit. After his parents both died, and in spite of having at least three siblings still living, he had little incentive to return for a visit. I expect that part of his attitude was a result of horror stories which some of his friends related based on their return visits to Seline after World War II when the Communists were in power. He often said that he wanted to remember his home through the eyes of a seventeen year-old youth with many fond memories.

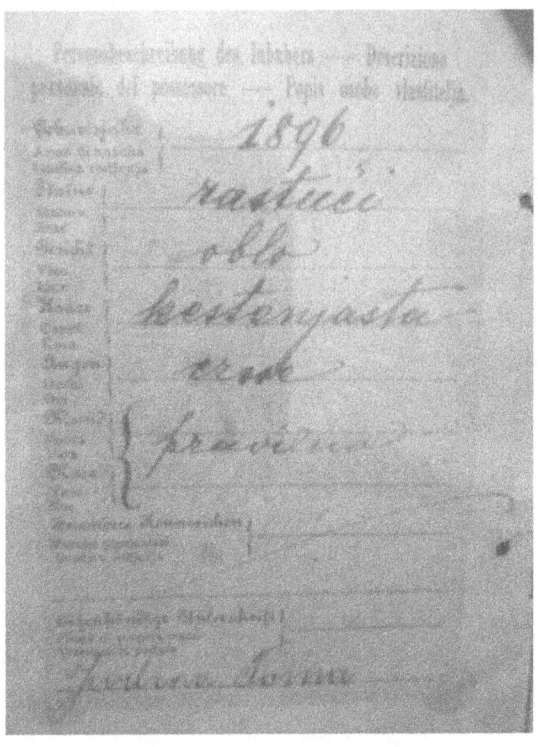

After leaving Ellis Island, he made his way to Donora, Pennsylvania with several friends ostensibly to visit a cousin. There were some families of Jurlinas there; however I have not been able to trace them thus far. Father was there only a short time and then headed west to Waterloo, Iowa to work on a railroad gang which was laying new track in the area. His first winter in Iowa was more than enough to make him look for a warmer climate and a decision to head east. Why he chose Cleveland, Ohio, is not known except for the existence of a rather large ethnic settlement of Croats and Slovenes in Cleveland.I had not visited my father's home or the home of my mother's parents at the first writing of this epistle. When I finally got to the point of being able to pay our way, a civil war erupted in Croatia and Bosnia-Hircegovina making a visit a rather risky business. In 1992, Mira Jurlina, eldest child of my cousin Ante Jurlina who lived in Zadar, moved to London and applied for protective asylum from the civil war in Croatia. In November 1992, Billie and I along with our son Michael and his wife Pamela flew to London to meet our young cousin for the first time. I had discovered Ante's existence just a few months before and had been exchanging letters with him and his family with his children, Mira, Anita and Marin, serving as translators. Sometime after 2003 we heard from Mira in a long letter in which she confided that she had had a relationship with a man from Australia which turned sour and she was trying to get over that. At this writing in April 2010 we have not heard a word from her since the last letter. I have tried to locate her but have not been successful. The British consul in Chicago did not offer any semblance of interest in our problem. We have not had a letter from Zadar or London for many years now (2011). Mira has not written to us and I assume that is the case because she is too involved with making a living and there may be another man in her life. I asked Milan Jurlina in Canada to make inquiries of Mira's father Ante on his next visit to Croatia (2010), but do not have an update.

OUR PARENTS AND HOW WE GOT ALONG

My parents must have been just like all the other parents in our ethnic neighborhood. One big difference in our parents was the fact that our mother was a native of Cleveland and she spoke English, whereas many mothers of my friends were immigrants from Europe and spoke very little English.

My mother worked hard all her life to try to give us children the advantages that she never had, such as a good education and a family life which did not revolve around the men in the family being pre-occupied with getting drunk on week-ends and having nothing to do with the children. She read a lot. That is, she tried to read the contemporary magazines and books that she was able to borrow from a few friends of hers. She took up playing the "Spanish Guitar" when she was about forty and I had given up on playing the "Hawaiian Steel Guitar" which almost all twelve-year olds in Cleveland were given the opportunity to take lessons.

Our mother always made sure that her children looked like they were from a home in which parents cared for their children. This was done by

making certain that we always went to school in freshly washed and pressed clothes even if we had been up late visiting with relatives or other guests in our home. Our mother had more concern about us than even she would admit to us - she cared but came from a background in which affection was not displayed. As well as I can remember, I never saw my parents kiss or embrace, not once. I am certain that both my parents loved the children a great deal but my mother showed that love more than my father. His display of affection of his children was even more difficult than it was for our mother. However, reflecting on that I am not certain that the experience of any of my contemporaries in our ethnic neighborhood was any different than ours. It seemed to me that affection, at least in our little world, was not for public display, not even that of parents with children.

Our family did spend evenings together most of the time until the children reached the teens. Radio programs such as AMOS & ANDY, STELLA DALLAS, JOHN'S OTHER WIFE, ONE MAN'S FAMILY, GEORGE BURNS & GRACIE ALLEN, JACK BENNY, etc. kept us close to the radio as a family, especially during the winter months. Mother did most of her crocheting while we listened to the radio programs, and Pop would read the newspaper while the children listened (sometimes the children were not too quiet). In those depression days, we got along with crystal radio sets that had earphones instead of loud speakers. All of the crystal sets were homemade and it was the early forties before we had a radio with a loudspeaker. That radio was an old Atwater Kent Radio that we salvaged from Aunt Frances garbage heap and it had to be repaired and babied to keep it working. Fortunately, my friend John Misic and I were deeply involved in radio, and John had many parts that he had salvaged from other junk radios, which we used as our source of repair materials.

Before the depression started, my father and mother had many friends in the Croatian Fraternal Union Lodge (C.F.U.) and at least once every week or so we would all walk to Gordon Park, about a mile from home, where the men would grill a small lamb on an open spit over a charcoal flame in a pit. In my childhood opinion, eating the well-done portion of the lamb was one of the most thrilling and satisfying experiences I could hope to have. After the depression was in full swing, the practice along with much visitation with friends outside the family ended. To this day, I am not certain why that had to change.

My father was not exposed to sports of any kind while he was growing up in Croatia and for that reason he was not involved in sports, even as a spectator, while I was playing baseball and football, etc. It was not until our youngest brother Bob starting playing baseball in the Class AA league that father went to see what was going on at the baseball diamond. Of course, the fact that Bob was a much better player than my brother Tom or I were must have had some influence on this action. Ha!

Discussions with my father centered about his experiences growing up in Croatia and his rather miserable living conditions on the side of the hill in an area which did not have much to offer for agriculture or anything else except fishing. I learned much later in life that only 25% of the land in Croatia is tillable and that mostly away from the Adriatic. My mother and I had long conversations, probably because I was her first and oldest child, about her growing up in a family in which her father made a living by owning and operating a saloon on East 61st Street north of St. Clair Avenue, not too far from 1157 East 63rd Street where I was born.

CITY BOY

Her father, as was previously noted, was murdered by two unknown assailants in late 1917 after the end of World War I. They simply walked into his saloon one night just before closing at midnight or so, and shot him and a friend with whom he was visiting at a table in front of the bar. My mother was a little over twelve years old at the time and the first to come down from their apartment over the saloon when the shots were heard. She climbed up on a whiskey barrel to reach the telephone so that she could dial and call the police. A picture of her in that position appeared in the local paper the next day. The murderers were never apprehended although the police were certain they were members of a gang operating along the waterfront of Lake Erie. Police theorized that my grandfather was silenced because he had operated as a police-informant reporting on names and conversations of the gang members who frequented his saloon.

My parents instilled in their children a work ethic that demanded that each individual had a responsibility to perform honest work for a living and had to have respect for law and order so that the society we live in would remain civilized and protect the freedoms for which early pioneers had fought. None of my parent's ancestors were involved in any way in the Revolutionary War or in any other conflict in these United States but they had a full appreciation of the sacrifices that had been made in their behalf; therefore, they expected us to live up to and protect our unearned heritage. The sense of right and wrong was instilled in us early on along with the knowledge that nothing was free and each person could take comfort in the fact that they were going to have to work for a living the rest of their lives. In addition, doing the job right and being loyal to your employer, friends and family was clearly taught. Finally, nobody that needs help should be denied the help of a true friend; sooner or later we all need help.

All in all I would have to say my mother was my best friend and counselor during my formative teens. She let me have my way as long as it was an honest and wholesome endeavor. She warned me about some of my friends whom she knew only by my conversation about them; however, she had a keen sense about people and those to be avoided. Fortunately, my friends were all pretty solid people.

Joseph Jurlina

OUR HOME AT 1157 EAST 63RD STREET

The Home of Thomas & Mary Jurlina family from 1922 until 1980
Located at 1157 East 63 rd Street in Cleveland, Cuyahoga County, Ohio
Birthplace of Joseph (1924), Edward (1925), Thomas (1927) & Robert (1929) Jurlina
Daughter Mary Jane (1941) was born in a Hospital

Mother and father married on 11 November 1922 in Cleveland, Cuyahoga County, Ohio and their first home was located at 1157 East 63rd Street. The house was new but located on half-a-lot that measured about forty by sixty feet - that is, 40 feet wide and 60 feet deep. Why this was allowed by the City of Cleveland I will never understand.

The house contained a kitchen with a small bedroom off the kitchen along with the only bathroom in the house. There was a dining room with a bedroom directly off this room along with a living room. There was an unfinished attic with one finished bedroom and a basement under about one-half of the first floor. How mother raised four children and accommodated a "border" I never will understand. The border was more important as an economic factor than any privacy we would have liked to have. I think I now (2010) understand that situation better having received a letter from a cousin who related how, at one time, in my father's home in Seline, Croatia there were 23 persons living in one house. I am not certain how many families that represented, but it must have been 4 5 at least - all Jurlinas and all just surviving.

CITY BOY

Our home was comfortable and reasonably well furnished until the depression came along and my father's wages dropped to four to six dollars a week. The mortgage on the home at the time was $5,200 incurred at the height of the "Roaring 20's", and the monthly mortgage-payments were twenty dollars ($20).

From an appearance standpoint the house was very attractive on the outside, but on the inside it was never designed to handle a family of six. It was not until I left home for service in the Army of the United State, and Tommy and Bobby were both in high school that they managed to finish the attic so that effectively there were three large bedrooms upstairs. The room at the front of the attic that had been my "laboratory" was untouched and maintained as it was when the house was built.

My "lab" was the site of many experiments with crystal sets and even multi-tube radios that I managed to learn how to construct from my close friend John J. Misic. How we managed to scrape together the parts for the radios I cannot now remember, except that I know we salvaged parts from junk piles of old radios at the local "City Dump". Actually in those days, Cleveland Sanitation Division collected trash in two different categories - combustible and non-combustible. The non-combustible was sent to the City Dump located along the lakefront between 40th and 55th Streets, while the combustible was incinerated somewhere else.

We frequented the City Dump in search for precious metals that we promptly sold to "Bill the Mayor", a hobo who made a living by buying and selling gold and silver. I said sold but as I look back on the situation we probably were paid a tenth of what the real value was at the time. To 10-12 year olds any amount seemed like a windfall because we could purchase two day-old Mrs. Wagner's pies for a nickel from the bakery located about 67th Street between St. Clair Avenue and the East/West NYC railroad tracks.

At the death of my father in 1979 my brother Bob, executor of the estate, sold our old home to a Slovenian emigrant family that had lived in the neighborhood for sometime. My father had lived in the home for almost fifty-seven (57) years - Mom and Pop lived in this home all of their married lives.

Joseph Jurlina

MY RELATIVES

My Aunts and Uncle, mother's sisters and her one brother, were all favorites of mine, probably because I was the first grandchild in the Telban family and they had no other baby to spoil until my brother Edward came along in June 1926, not quite two years after I was born in 1924. The Telban children, in order of birth, were: Mary my mother, born 20 June 1904; Anna born 5 August 1907; Frances, born 19 October 1909; Josephine, born 10 March 1912; Angela, born 6 August 1914; and John, born 7 September 1916.

Grandmother married a second time, after her first husband was murdered in 1917, to John Jeric, another product of Slovenia. To that marriage was born one child, Julia Jeric, born 10 November 1922, the day before my mother and father were married on 11 November 1922. Grandmother Mary Novak Telban Jeric could not attend the wedding because of having the new baby, Aunt Julia.

Aunt Anna Telban Avenmarg, born 5 August 1907, was always very friendly and interested in my well-being when she saw me but she married in 1925, about a year after I was born; therefore, I saw her only on special occasions in my early childhood but more often when her son and

WILLIAM & ANNA AVENMARG WEDDING – 8 AUGUST 1925
WITH THOMAS & MARY JURLINA

daughter, William and Elizabeth, were about 8-10 years old and I could visit them in their home. I distinctly remember the Uncle Ray Avenmarg who lived with my Aunt and her husband for a while. Raymond Otto Avenmarg was born in 1909, about four years after his brother William was born. Raymond was a seaman on a Lake Erie freighter while I knew him. He chewed tobacco like it was chewing gum. As I recall he had false teeth at an early age and when he had a mouth full of chew, but minus his teeth, he could screw up his face to look like "Popeye the Sailor", a favorite of all of the children of our day. Since starting this narrative and being involved in family genealogy I discovered for the first time that Ray married in 1943, about three months after I left home for services in the Army of the USA. Aunt Anna married William Carl Hermann Avenmarg in 1925 and they had three children: William George, born in 1926; Elizabeth Mae born in 1928; and Richard James, born in 1931. Uncle Bill Avenmarg always scared us Jurlina-kids to death with his loud kidding around and his large chew of tobacco like his brother Ray. He was always very gentle and must have loved us dearly to put up with us in those days when we were under his feet all the time. Uncle Bill worked for the Buckeye Brass Co. as did his father before him. Aunt Anna died in 1974 at the age of 67 years and Uncle Bill died in 1951 at the age of 46.

MARY TELBAN JURLINA & ANNA TELBAN AVENMARG JASKO — ABT 1940

Aunt Frances Telban Simoncic, born 19 October 1909, was always very interested in my activities and my well-being, more so than my other Aunts. This was probably because after her marriage she lived within a block of our home on Orton Court. I was five when she married, and while pregnant she spent a lot of time with my mother, her oldest sister, and our family. Genevieve Simoncic, Aunt Fanny's only child was born in 1931 and I can remember sitting with Genevieve while she was no more than two years old (I must have been all of seven at the time) while Aunt Fanny visited her in-laws across the street.

FRANCES, GENEVIEVE & JOSEPH SIMONCIC – ABOUT 1943

Aunt Fanny married Joseph J. Simoncic in 1929. He grew up just down the street from our home (four houses North and on the same side of 63rd Street) but I never knew much of him until he married my Aunt and starting being our family barber during the depression which started that year. I do not recall whether my father could have paid Uncle Joe or just traded barbering for a supply of wine and/or whiskey that my father was making during prohibition days. In fact, all of my Uncles would imbibe when they had occasion to visit our home, but back to Uncle Joe. He was the local Democratic Precinct Chairman I believe, because he always had much to do at election time and the politicians were always calling him for favors. It was his job to make certain everybody eligible to vote did vote for the Democratic candidates of "his" choice, that is, he told the folks how to vote for the best man. I often wondered how he could get away with that kind of activity without getting hurt - but he did. I recall he and several of the neighbors had a place where they played poker on a regular basis. Aunt Frances died in 1961 at age 52 years with a breast cancer. She died in October after my mother died in June 1960 of lung cancer. Joseph died in 1954 at age 48.

FRED & JOSEPHINE ZERULL WEDDING ON 17 NOV. 1934 WITH FRANCES & JOHN TELBAN

COUSINS JOAN & MARGARET ZERULL ABT 1950-1951

Aunt Josephine, born 10 March 1912, married Frederick Zerull in 1934 and their first home was the front upstairs bedroom of our house where they stayed for a short time. Fritz, as we called him, was born in East Prussia in 1908. They had two girls Margaret and Joan born in 1942 and 1944 respectively. I had very little contact with Margaret and Joan since I was inducted in the Army in March 1943 and having stayed in Texas for most of their growing up days. I knew very little about either of the girls. Uncle Fred and Aunt Josephine both worked for the Buckeye Brass Company. Aunt Josephine died on 29 December 2002 in Euclid, Ohio at the age of 90. Fred Zerull died in 1958 at the age of fifty, because of a heart problem.

UNCLE WALTER AND WIFE AUNT ANGELA PASTWA ABOUT 1937

Aunt Angela Telban, born 6 August 1914, married Walter Pastwa in 1934. Walter was born in Cleveland in 1911, and died in 1961 at age 59, of a liver problem. They had one child Walter, Jr., born in 1935 and died in 1936 of hydro encephalitis (water on the brain). I cannot now remember where Walter worked but it must have been close to home and in the area between East 40th and 60th Streets near the lakefront. Aunt Angela, it seemed to me, spent a very lonely married life after her son died. It seemed that whenever I saw her, her husband was nowhere to be seen. I recall someone saying that Walter may have held Angela responsible for the death of the only child. Walter died at age 50 after a life of drinking too much. Aunt Angela died on Easter Sunday 1992 at age 78, after complaining about abdominal problems that turned out to be gallstones and/or other problem with gall bladder function. Aunt Angela wanted to help me earn pocket money when I was a teenager so she would often have me do chores for her for which she paid me some nominal sum. Scrubbing floors in Cleveland was always a chore to be avoided so that was one of the things that I did most along with the washing of windows. She never had much extra money so I knew she was making a sacrifice just to be of some help to me. It was obvious that while I was home (before going off to the service in March 1943) she made me one of her favorites.

CITY BOY

Uncle John J. Telban, born 7 September 1916, married Theresa Maric in 1935. He was aged 19 and Theresa was aged 17. They had four children: Delores, born 1935; Theresa, born 1937; John Jr., born 1940; and Ronald, born 1947. Uncle John had a tough early childhood because of his illnesses. He was diagnosed with tuberculosis when he was quite young and spent a short time in a fresh-air sanitarium. Also, I was led to believe, he had a heart murmur that may have been the result of a previous illness. In spite of all these impediments, Uncle John was a very talented person and by the time I left home for the service he was known for his ability as an electrician, a master plumber, a master welder, an expert at furnace and air conditioning installations. In short, he was a very handy person and could make all the money he had time and desire to make. Unfortunately, he also liked to drink alcoholic beverages and spent much time and money in that pursuit in spite of suggestions from his sisters and other family members to refrain. My contact with Uncle John was somewhat limited in my early life because he was eight years older than I was. John J. Telban was inducted into the Army shortly after I was in spite of his early health problems, his wife and three children. Not only that but he was in the fight around the Burma Road within 3-4 months after leaving home. He stayed there for the duration of the war. Being a jack-of-all-trades made him very valuable person to the hospital group to which he was assigned late in the war. He talked about making beds for the army hospital nurses in his outfit. After WWII, I saw him only on those trips to Cleveland that I was able to make on my way back to Dallas from New York City or other points east where I had been on business. On those occasions, Uncle John was very friendly and quite interested in what my family was doing in Texas. It was almost to the point that I could detect a bit of longing on his part to get away from the big city environment. He never admitted that directly but that is the feeling I received from his conversation. Interestingly enough, when I was in his presence he did very little serious drinking. I do not know whether he did this in deference to my known dislike for big drinkers or because he was already having some serious health problems. He died in 1974 at the age of fifty-eight.

Joseph Jurlina

My Aunt Julia Jeric, daughter of Grandma and her second husband Frank Jeric, born on 10 November 1922, was always close to me because she was only two years older than I. Julia was a very nervous individual with many health problems of which I knew little. My mother was always partial to her young sister probably because Julia was just two years older than I was. Mother could never quite understand why Julia had so many upsetting problems.

JULIA JERIC LASCO & DAD FRANK JERIC – 1940

The source of the problems could very well have been the fact that Grandma and Uncle Frank did not get along too well and they finally divorced in 1936 when Julia was only fourteen years old. Uncle Frank died in 1943 a very broken man, which probably also contributed to Julia's reported rather hostile relationship with her kin by blood and marriage. Julia and I always had a good and friendly relationship most probably because I was gone after March 1943.

Julia married Charles Lasco in May 1941 and they had two children: Charles Frank born and died in July 1943 and David born 14 June 1956. Julia died with a heart attack on 2 August 1969 at an age just short of forty-seven years. Charles "Skeezix" Lasco was always a very outgoing and friendly individual who enjoyed life to the fullest and never had a negative thought. He was an excellent bowler having several perfect "300" games to his credit. He served in the 82nd Airborne Division and saw much action during the Battle of the Bulge in WWII. Apparently, he

CITY BOY

served in several airborne divisions in the area of the Bulge. He was a very friendly individual who often visited my parents even after the death of his wife Julia. He died in 2004 at the age of eighty seven.

JULIA JERIC LASCO, DAVID & FATHER CHARLES "SKEEZIX" LASCO – ABOUT 1960

RELATIONSHIPS WITH AUNTS AND UNCLES

*My closest relationship with relatives would have to include my Aunts Frances, Josephine, Anna, and Angela. I had much more contact with my Aunt Frances, or Fannie as she was called, because for all my growing up days she lived just a block down the street on Orton Court with her husband Joseph Simoncic and eventually her only child Genevieve. My cousin Genevieve was born when I was about seven and by the time I was ten or twelve I was the official baby sitter for her. Although I did not sit too long I was honored that anyone would give me such a responsibility.

Aunt Josephine, or Peppie as we called her, was born in 1912, only twelve years older than I. She was always one of the best natured and jovial but dry-witted members of the Telban family. For a short time after her marriage to Fred Zerull they lived in our upstairs bedroom. Fred used to entertain us by playing his piano-accordian, an instrument that he played by ear - he never had a music lesson in his life. Only Margie and Joannie, my Aunt Peppie and Uncle Fred visited in our home frequently. This was probably due to the fact my mother was Peppie's oldest sister and with whom there was a very good relationship. Peppie always treated me as her equal, or at least that's the way I felt about the way she respected my teenage reactions to everything.

Anna Telban Avenmarg was the mother of cousins William, Elsie and Richard. Because of her children Aunt Annie had the pleasure of my company for many days at a time when the children were not in school. The Avenmarg's lived just about four blocks from our home with much more yard than we had at our place. As far as I am aware the Avenmarg's did not own the home but rented it from the time I can recall visiting there until after I left home in 1943 to enter the service. We never spent much time in their home probably because we made too much noise but we were always welcome to come to visit with the Avenmarg cousins. Raymond Otto Avenmarg, Annie's brother-in-law, lived with Bill and Anna Avenmarg for some time as I recall. Ray worked for a company that operated lake-freighters on Lake Erie. He was quite comical when he removed his false teeth and curled down his lip to look like Popeye. He chewed tobacco and it seemed he always had a wad of tobacco about two inches in diameter in his mouth. The fear of having him miss what he was spitting at made you very cautious when you were standing nearby. Ray married in 1945, about six weeks after Billie and I did, at the age of about thirty-six to a lady about twelve years his junior.

Aunt Angela, or Angie as we called her, was ten years older than I was, but she too treated me as though I were her age. In spite of that, in conversation within our family she always referred to me as Joey or Little Joey. Some how with Angela it never made any difference what she called me. While I was in high school I saw Aunt Angela every Friday of the year because it was my permanent job to scrub her kitchen floors for the lavish earning of twenty-five cents. Of course, it did not take long to scrub the floor and besides that Angela needed someone with whom to have conversation. Her husband Walter Pastwa was always so busy visiting down at the local saloon he did not have time for his wife. My parents decided that Walter blamed Angela for the death of their only child Walter Junior who died from hydro-encephalitis, or some such problem. Needless to say, my respect for Walter was not what it could have been.

John J. Telban, or Johnny as we called him, was born 7 September 1916, the last child by my grandfather John J. Telban. Johnny was a very interesting individual with many talents. He was a good electrician, plumber, tinsmith and many natural abilities. My contact with him was interrupted in March 1943 when I entered the army.

OUR FAMILY TRADITIONS AND SPECIAL FOODS

I cannot recall any special family traditions; however, it was always great fun to have all the relatives visit in our home for those special occasions of baptisms, weddings, Easter, Thanksgiving, and Christmas. I am not certain why the gatherings took place at our home for the most part, but it might have been related to the fact that my father, in the times he could afford the grapes, made two or three barrels of wine which he was want to share with anyone who would help him drink the wine, this in addition to the aforementioned whiskey making endeavor.

After the depression really took hold, only close members of the family met on holidays to break what little bread there was to break. Again, these get-togethers took place at our home more than likely because my mother was the oldest child of the children of John Telban children and married longest.

An old European custom, which carried over to the States by the Croatians in Cleveland during the feast of the Passover involved placing some fresh blood of a lamb on the upper part of a doorway used most frequently in the home. I seem to recall one occasion this was done by a priest of St. Paul's Roman Catholic Church while my younger brother Edward was critically ill. Edward died a few days later. I do not remember this being done again. Now I wonder whether this was a dream or an actual experience.

Family birthdays and anniversaries were not a big thing in our family that I can recall. It seems that on the nearest Sunday to our birthday some mention or even a toast was offered to the person or persons celebrating a birthday. According to some European customs, the date of Christian baptism or the patron saints day of your namesake was celebrated. My father didn't remember my birthday too well but he always remembered that St. Joseph's day was 19th of March and called or wrote postcards recalling that date while I was in the Army.

I do not remember my parents celebrating the anniversary of their marriage and, in fact, when I was a teenager I had to press them for the actual date. It seemed to me that while Europeans had many customs, the celebration of wedding anniversaries was not a popular one, and if so was done very privately because I do not recall any such celebrations during my growing up days. Since I probably had other things on my mind I may have just missed the occasions. Besides, if you had no extra cash you celebrated in a very "quiet way".

Mealtime in our family was always a serious business because for many years there was not an abundance of food. During the week, my father and mother had their breakfast of coffee and toast together early in the A.M. because my father usually left home for work about 5:45 A.M. to catch a bus about three blocks away. The children had their breakfast together an hour or so later. Father carried his lunch to work and the children always came home from elementary school and ate with mother. Those children in High School always fended for themselves but I do not recall having any large lunch.

Evening meals were generally done as a family but were not formal gatherings. I am certain that my parent's home-experiences with meals in their homes were not formal affairs where any serious discussions took place. That is my recalled experience. Mealtime for many years was pretty meager and I often wondered how mother managed to survive on the amount she ate, and how my father managed to maintain his energy level with what he had to eat. For many years during the depression, the dinner we had to share was soup or a goulash made with animal organs such as: heart, kidney, and liver. For the most part mother made vegetable soups from beef bones that still had a little meat attached. After meals the children usually played together while the parents read the newspaper when there was one to read, or talked about events of interest in the other relative's families.

Family photographs were practically nonexistent in our growing up years. Very few cameras were ever seen in our neighborhood or in our relative's families. As a result, only a few pictures remain of our growing up days. Not until my brother Tom and I started taking pictures with some worn out Brownie Kodak cameras did we gather many pictures of our family. My parents did not enjoy being photographed because they were so self-conscious of what they called "shabby clothes". For many years during my early childhood, all members of the family had only one change of "Sunday" clothes, and my mother's clothes were always the oldest. This was also the reason mother and father did not attend Church on a regular basis because they felt they could not dress appropriately for such occasions. At least that was the excuse used and probably quite true.

ELEMENTARY EDUCATION OF JURLINA CHILDREN IN CLEVELAND, OHIO

My elementary education, as well as that of all my siblings, started in the parish school of St. Vitus Roman Catholic Church located in the 6100 block of Glass Avenue in Cleveland, Ohio. This Church was started about 1893 in a wooden structure on 61st Street facing east just north of Glass Avenue. The Church is in existence at this writing of May 2010, and in fact, St. Vitus Parish is probably in better financial shape at this writing than it ever was while I was in school. A very significant number of the present parishioners have been members all their lives - and many were my classmates from 1930-1938.

The original Church was a wooden structure that I recall attending services in for a couple of years after I started first grade. The present brick church structure, on the corner of 61st and Glass Avenue faces south on Glass Avenue, was started in 1930 and completed in 1932. In 1993 the

Joseph Jurlina

Church was refurbished and redecorated to look very much like the Churches in Slovenia, the origin of many of the founders and present members who have come to Cleveland to make their American homes.

The Parish School was originally staffed with Sisters of Notre Dame, who were housed in a house on Glass Avenue and 61st Street, directly across the street from the school building. I do not recall ever knowing exactly how many Nuns there were at any one time but I would think there were at least eight and possibly ten while I was in school. As I recall the classes were relatively small consisting of about 20 students. I believe our elementary school education was as fine as any available in Cleveland, Ohio at that time. The school was closed about 2000.

My brothers Thomas John and Robert Stephen were at St. Vitus for part of the time I was there. I was in the third grade when Thomas started school and I was in the sixth grade when Robert started school. The older children usually had recess apart from the younger children and as a result, I rarely saw my brothers on the playground during recess. We usually went home together for lunch and always went to school together. In fact, one winter morning when the ground was covered with several inches of snow my brother Tom found several dollar bills on the snow in front of the Spech grocery store. Bob found some also. Unfortunately, I only found one while both Bob and Tom found three or four each. That experience made me more aware of what was on the ground between home and school but to no avail for I did not find anything of value after that experience.

My best friends at St. Vitus were two boys that I thought were the smartest kids in the school. The first was George Ozanich, a boy who was good looking and what I thought was in great physical shape. We never had much in common but I always admired the way he handled himself in the classroom and on the playground. The second was Albert James Anthony Vidmar, as he always identified himself. Al and I were great buddies and rivals all at the same time. He was a natural artist but was color-blind so he always "buddied up" with me and me with him on art-projects. He did the hard work and I helped to be his worst critic and advisor as to coloring and shading, especially on drawings done with chalk on the blackboard. Al and I stayed together through high school where he ended up third in a graduating class of over four hundred following James Burns and another fellow whose name I cannot now recall. The best I could do in that case was twenty-eighth which I thought was rather pathetic compared to Al and James.

Our grade school classes were rather unique because we did not have a bully in any of them in spite of the fact that we had several "older" boys in the classes that had been held back a class or two. I always enjoyed most of my classes in grade school and looked forward to getting into the classroom each day. Winter days were especially nice since the rooms were always very warm and not drafty as it was at home on those bitter cold days of winter along Lake Erie.

All of the Nuns were great teachers but I think I liked two best of all. Sister Athenasia taught me how to read so I always felt that she had opened the doors of knowledge to me and as a result I really thought she hung the moon; however, as I passed on to the third grade I met Sister Frumenza. She was also my sixth or seventh grade teacher and was eager to make a student out of all the boys in her classes. It seemed that the girls pretty much set the pace, with a few notable exceptions like Al Vidmar, and she encouraged the rest of us to match wits so to speak. She wanted us to realize that although all problems in the world could not be solved. She also spent a lot of time pointing out, how people of the past had demonstrated with inventions and developments that many problems could be solved.

Math, geography and artistic projects were our favorite subjects and probably in that order. All the teachers pitted the boys against the girls in all the subjects only to discover that the girls did best in everything but math. The girls excelled in anything that required instant recall but the boys always did better in those subjects that required some logic.

In reviewing those school activities to which our children and grandchildren were exposed while in grade school, my contemporaries and I really missed a lot because we had no choral groups or singing of any kind. We had no plays or bit-part acting to test our talents. Spelling bees were the only real challenges presented and I always assumed that that was a result of the public spelling bees put on by the local newspapers. Of course, no one that I knew, including me ever made it to the final competitions where some publicity was given to the school. It seemed that most of the winners came from the public school children. It may well be that the Roman Catholic Schools did not encourage participation in the contests on a city-wide school versus public school basis but kept the competition within each school. That would be much simpler and probably the rational used.

My brothers and I walked to school each day because it was only the equivalent of two long blocks and in those days automobiles were not the danger they are today. As I recall there was only one family along the entire two block area that owned an automobile and they worked nights so the car presented very little danger to the children walking or playing in the streets. The biggest obstacle in getting to school was in the winter when the snow might be two feet deep, but that never kept us from school, it just made us arrive a little late and wet because of all the romping in the snow which took place. Discipline for me was always a problem, or at least it seems to me I had problems by virtue of the number of times I had the back of my hands spanked for misbehaving. My problem revolved around my cousin Josephine Bizil who was assigned the seat in front of me. She had long brown hair that just had to be messed with and I did. On several occasions I twisted the ends of her tresses together and then dipped them into the inkwells we had on our desks. Those tresses made some of the most interesting designs on paper - evidence of which was not easy to destroy once the teacher got suspicious that something was taking place that cousin did not like. Punishment varied from teacher to teacher but for the most part it consisted of spanking the back of the hand with a ruler, a severe reprimand in the cloak room, blackboard cleaning duty after school, and standing in the corner while the fun things were being done in the classroom. Josephine died in 1979.

CHILDHOOD FRIENDS AND ACTIVITIES

Practically all of my childhood friends were also the children who were in school and church with me because we all grew up in the same neighborhood. Roman Catholic Parishes were very particular about all the children in the parish going to the same parochial school. My siblings and I had very few friends outside our immediate neighborhood because we rarely traveled outside the neighborhood. The friends I can now recall, most of whom may be deceased include the following: Albert James Anthony Vidmar, with whom I went through all grades of school through high school. He was mentioned previously as an artist and exceptionally smart student. Al died about 1988 just a few months before our 50th anniversary reunion of graduates from the eighth grade at St. Vitus Roman Catholic Elementary School.

George Ozanich was also one of the smartest students and a good friend through the first eight grades. I lost touch with George after Junior High School and did not see him again until our 1988 St. Vitus 8th Grade Reunion. He now lives in Redwood, California and maintains contact via the Internet.

Margaret Jacknik was a pretty girl who always seemed to enjoy making me uncomfortable during recess periods with her barbs about not making a perfect grade on all tests. She was one of the smartest girls of the class. The last time I saw Margaret was about 1960 as I was on the Rapid Transit traveling from the airport to my parent's home. She was married and as I

Joseph Jurlina

JOSEPH JURLINA IN FIRST ROW FROM TOP & THIRD FROM THE RIGHT EIGHT GRADE GRADUATION JUNE 1938
ST. VITUS R.C. SCHOOL IN CLEVELAND, OHIO

recall she and her husband had several children. She was always very attractive to me; however, I did nothing to develop any relationship nor did she make any advances. If she did, maybe I did not recognize one, ha!

Some of the neighborhood kids included: Ray Simon who was killed pretty soon after December 7, 1941 while serving in the Marine Corps at the age of seventeen; Ray Brown, the son of a roofer and ex-navy person; Raymond and Norbert Novak; Nick Fumic, also; Frank Popotnik, who was a year or so younger than I; Rudolph something; Fred Baron, now deceased also; Johnny Zorich, now deceased also; Toots something who, lost his leg during WWII; John J. Misic who introduced me to the world of Amateur Radio and radio in general, and ultimately led me to study electrical engineering about which I had previously known nothing. There were many others with whom I spent much time playing baseball, football, kick- the-can and whatever else happened to be the fad. There were two boys my age, whose names I cannot recall, who were killed while riding double on a bicycle through the intersection of St. Clair and 65th Street. The driver of the bicycle tried to beat a streetcar through the intersection and did not make it but hit the streetcar about in the mid-section. Both boys slid under the streetcar and were killed instantly. It was a very traumatic experience for all of us at the age of 10-12 for we all thought we were invincible and smarter than any adult around because we had already passed the grade level achieved by most of the adults with the exception of my mother.

CHILDHOOD CHORES & FIRST JOB

The childhood chores that stand out most of all include: shoveling coal into the coal bins two or three times a year and keeping the furnace fire banked during the time my father was not at home; scrubbing the kitchen floor at least once a week at home and for my Aunt Angela but she paid me a quarter of a dollar; helping my mother do the laundry for her sisters; washing dishes until my siblings were old enough to do that for Mom.

We did not receive an allowance as such because for most of our growing-up lives there was not that kind extra cash around; however, my mother

Joseph Jurlina

Mary Telban Jurlina, With Sons About 1932-1933
Joseph, oldest at abt. Nine Years, Thomas J. at abt. Six Years
Robert S. at abt. Four Years

found a nickel or a dime every once in a while so that we could take in the local western movie.

When I reached the age of about thirteen, I took on delivery of the Cleveland Shopping News, a local merchant paper delivered at no cost to the families, paid for by the advertisers. The 400+ customer route consisting of our 3-4 block neighborhood was delivered by 7am at least twice a week and in the busy holiday seasons as many as four times a week. Each paper had to be fastened to the front door, or another specified by the customer, with green rubber bands supplied by the employer. If any papers were "porched", the carrier was dismissed without question. Of course, during the time of the depression jobs were hard to come by so compliance was expected and a matter of course. On average it took a wagon loaded with paper to cover the route and from the start required anywhere from 45 minutes to 70 minutes to finish the deliveries. The winter deliveries were always the worst. My very first delivery was made in about January 1940 at 5:00 am when the temperature was about 6 degrees above zero

CITY BOY

Fahrenheit and snowing. Stubborn me, I refused to wear a hat. Needless to say, on the second delivery I was better clothed with a knit cap over my ears. Brother Tom was nice enough to help as he aged and then Bob did the same and assisted me. It was always our aim as a duo to get the job done in less than 20 minutes or so. The pay for our services at first was sixty-five cents per delivery for the first 2-3 years and in the final years was up to about ninety-five cents per delivery. It was not much but it did help pay the bills and even purchased much-needed reading glasses for all three boys. A neighbor had "owned" the route for at least 4 years before me and I handed it down to my brother Tom and then to my brother Bob - which means we had the route controlled for at least 9 years.

I'll never forget that the first fifteen dollars I saved from the paper route went to buy a desk on which most of my studying took place. In fact, on Monday 8 December 1941, during my Junior year of High School I was working on a lab report at that desk, when I heard the broadcast from Washington D.C. of President Franklin Delano Roosevelt's speech to Congress asking for a declaration of war against Japan for the bombing at Pearl Harbor. In March of 1943 I would join that

JOSEPH JURLINA WITH BROTHER THOMAS JOHN AT AGES 8 & 5

war being inducted into the Army and asked to report to Camp Perry, Ohio for processing and indoctrination.

The Jurlina sons had to have a job to help support the family during the period from 1940 until after the war ended in 1945, a time of very bad economics for the family. My father, as a laborer, had to work very hard through the "depression years" just to provide minimum food, housing and subsistence requirements for a family of two adults and four children. I suppose it was fortunate for Bob, Tom and me that we had this wonderful opportunity to learn about responsibility of maintaining a job and supporting the family in our small way. Our route helped us to make enough money to take care of personal needs and the rest went into the family coffers.

Delivering the Shopping News and keeping up with our studies was a given. We never thought about not getting the best grades we could - that was a fundamental requirement of all "Catholic Hunkies" as relatives and friends called us. It was assumed every child would do his/her best to get a "good" education so that something other than a common laborer's job would be the ultimate result.

MY SIBLINGS - OUR DAYS TOGETHER BEFORE & AFTER THE ARMY AND WWII

My siblings and I played together very well until I reached an age when my mother would trust me to go off to play with my friends. Although there was not that much an age difference, except with my sister, in that time there was enough difference in the age of my siblings that we had little in common. We have come closer over the years but the miles of separation have made a close-tie almost impossible. The death of my brother Tom was a severe blow because he died at such a young age (39) and left a wife and three very young children.

There was always an understanding among us children that we were a family and one child's problem was everyone's problem. It was understood that we were all for one and one for all. Being the oldest child, I had more of a parental role to follow than I sometimes wanted. My brothers inherited all my hand me downs, such as they were.

CITY BOY

Invariably I was hard on the clothes but mother managed to salvage enough from mine to keep Tom and Bob both looking pretty good for poor folks. Of course, we didn't know that you had a choice in what you wore. We wore what there was to wear and didn't ask questions because we knew pretty much what the answer would be when asked.

Tommy, Bobby and I always walked to school together because it was the responsibility of the older brother to get the younger boys there especially while we were all enrolled at St. Vitus Parochial School through the Eighth Grade. I was three years older than Tommy and five years older than Bobby so the difference in age became more acute when I reached the Eighth Grade. That is where the divergence of opinions seem to start - after all, I was in Junior High School. Ha! The best part of having brothers manifested itself during those miserable cold winter days when you had to stay indoors. You were never really alone because there were always a couple of brothers you could play with in the attic or basement.

ROBERT STEPHEN JURLINA – ABT 1932

The worst part of having brothers was sharing everything, although there was not much to share. Tommy and Bobby were always ready to help their big brother and as they grew older made delivering the News an easy task. They succeeded me as the carrier of record and as a result the

Jurlina boys had that route in the family for ten years or more. I do not recall who inherited the route from Bobby after Tommy and I moved out of the picture.

THOMAS JURLINA WITH DAUGHTER MARY JANE ABT 1942

Mary Jane came along when I was seventeen years old and only about fifteen months before I left home for the army in 1943. She had many problems with croup and other things that kept her crying much of her first two years to the point where when I left home in 1943 it was a great relief to get away from the "crying child". Unfortunately, I did not get to watch her grow up as I was away from home from March 1943 until the fall of 1950 when Billie, Carol Ann and I moved to Cleveland from McCamey, Texas, but more about that later.

As I may have mentioned elsewhere, all the Jurlina boys were good students in school, because our mother did not tolerate "bad-grades" or improper deportment. She thought we should enjoy the learning process and fully expected that we would try our best in the schooling process. I believe even as young as we were, we recognized from what went on about us during the depression that an education was important and a crucial element to getting employment. Even though jobs were scarce mother thought that we would be more competitive in the market place with a good primary and secondary education. College was never a consideration in our family because no one in the family had ever made it to college so that was never discussed.

Personalities in the Jurlina male-family were quite varied. Tommy was the comedian, joker and artist of the family and ended up majoring in mechanical engineering at what was then Case Institute of Technology. Bobby was the athlete of the family and played baseball like a pro but never got the timing right for him to get into the pro ranks. The threat of being drafted if he quit his defense job at Republic Steel hung over him until he finally enlisted in the Army and ended up in Japan as part of the occupation troops. I was the student and after discharge from the Army of the U.S.A. I attended the University of Texas in Austin as an electrical engineering student under the GI Bill and managed to get my Batchelor of Science degree in January of 1950. I believe my graduation from college was the first in the Ohio clan.

My siblings and I have gotten along better as we all have aged in spite of the long distance between the Texas Jurlinas and the Ohio Jurlinas. Before my brother Thomas died in 1967, he and I had developed what I would describe as a very close relationship and a better understanding of each other than we had previously had. In his last days, he asked that I look after his family, especially his wife Leona, who he felt could not handle their three children and her relationship with her parents and her siblings, especially her brother Leonard. That has been harder than I would have liked because of the distance. On the other hand, I believe Bob and Mary Jane have accepted the Texas Jurlinas as kin and close friends. It is sad that we do not live much closer together but that distance is a fact-of-life which we try to accept.

MARY JANE ELAM, GENEVIEVE WARD, JOE, ELSIE YECK & BOB BILLIE JURLINA

It was a real joy when my brother Bob and sister Mary Jane came to our 60th celebration in 2005 as did my cousins Elsie Yeck and Genevieve Ward. November of that same year, Tom (my brother Tom's son) came to visit with his wife, Mary, and children, Merielle and Peter. At thanksgiving the following year we were able to celebrate Thanksgiving with them at our granddaughter, Katherine's house in New York. Mary Jane's daughter Jennifer also came up from NYC to dine with us. In 2009 we also enjoyed the regular company and assistance of Edward Baznik (the eldest son of our neice, Linda, my brother Tom's daughter) while he lived and worked in Dallas at his first post-graduate position as a structural engineer.

CITY BOY

MY HOMETOWN - CLEVELAND, CUYAHOGA COUNTY, OHIO

As far as we were concerned, the world was just like our neighborhood - that is, made up of neighborhoods of people whose second language was English. I could not communicate with most of the adults in our neighborhood because I could not speak Slovenian, Croatian, Polish, German or Russian - the languages of the neighborhood. Therefore, my English conversation contact with adults was limited to my parents and teachers, most of who did not originate or live in our neighborhood. The notable exceptions were my Mom and her four sisters, one brother, and one stepsister who had the same growing up experience.

Cleveland is located on the south shore of Lake Erie and when I lived there it was one of the most significant large industrial cities in the country. It was a proverbial melting pot of people from all points of the globe but predominantly from central Europe. The neighborhood in which I grew up was an ethnic Slovenian neighborhood with a sprinkle of Croatians and one or two Russian families, but not to many blocks to the east one could find a Polish settlement and the same distance to the west, a Croatian neighborhood. This latter area was where my father settled when he first came to Cleveland, and also the reason all the boys in our family were baptized in St. George Roman Catholic Church on East 40th street. No black families lived within 4-5 blocks of our neighborhood.

The soil of Cleveland close to the lake was very sandy down to depths beyond the concern of the average homeowner. The house we lived in had only a partial basement, that is, about half of the area under the house was excavated. Anytime we needed sand for making cement, all we had to do was take a shovel into the area under the front of the house and shovel out what we needed.

The sandy soil and proximity to the lake was just what the hardwood forest of the area thrived on - there were all kinds of trees, many of which grew to be over one hundred feet tall. A "Black Oak" tree that was growing in Gordon Park, about a mile from home, was at least six feet in diameter three feet above ground. It was one of the most beautiful trees I had ever seen. Unfortunately, when the Interstate Highway system was developed in the late 1950's this large tree, along with many hundreds of others, was removed from the landscape.

Generally, the terrain along the lake was flat but the further away from the lake in all three directions it gradually changes to gently rolling tree-covered hills. The further one goes from the lake the land becomes more "loamy" and the soil on the hills becomes more shallow and covers the rocks rolled up by the advancing glaciers in time past.

Cleveland, Ohio is not known for its mild climate. Winters are long with first snowfall by the second week in November, and some of these first snowfalls can be memorable. For example, in the winter of 1950-51 Billie, Carol Ann and I were getting ready to celebrate Carol Ann's fourth birthday on 25 November so we ordered a cake for delivery on her birthday. On the evening of the 24th, it started snowing and by the night of the 25th we had had almost 42 inches of snow that shut the city down for almost two weeks. Interestingly, the forecast for that period was for "snow flurries"; therefore, all the city snow removal equipment was parked in parking lots that were not accessible for days after the snowfall.

The spring, summer and fall seasons are remarkable because they are all so distinct and different than the winters. Spring is especially beautiful because of the many fruit trees that give exceptional displays of blossoms each year. Summer is not the best but passable even with high humidity because the temperatures are rather mild, often 90 degrees or less but with an occasional 95+ high and with high humidity. The fall has to be as spectacular as the spring but often is rather variable in length. Early winters can cut short a very enjoyable fall to the point that leaf raking may be put off until the following spring.

The 1940 U.S. Census had Cleveland with a population of about 900,000. Just before I left home for the Army in March of 1943, it seemed that people started to move to the suburbs to get away from the smog and coal-soot covered area in which I grew up. If I remember correctly the population of Cleveland by the 2000 U.S. Census was less than 450,000. Apparently, this same thing happened in every industrial metropolitan area of the mid-west. The 2010 Census should reveal more details of the population decline.

The suburbs and rural areas, not too far from our home, were beautiful and clean by comparison. As children, we often talked about moving to the suburbs when we were out of school and settled in a "good" job. Of course, Mom and Pop never made it out of the neighborhood - Mom died in 1960 and Pop in 1979 while they were permanent residents at 1157 East 63rd Street in the home which they purchased in 1922, the year they married.

The suburb that really fascinated us children was Bratenahl which is an area one mile from north to south located just east of Gordon Park, from about 76th Street to 105th more or less. The population of Bratenahl was never very high because it was made up of relatively large landed residential sites. Current population is less than 2,000 souls so I would expect it was always smaller than that when we were enjoying its one tree-lined boulevard that traversed the City east to west through the center of the suburb. Essentially, the City was made up of large estates along Lake Erie on the north and south sides of this boulevard. When we were between the ages of 10-13, we often walked along the beautiful boulevard just enjoying the natural beauty. A good many times we ended up walking completely through the suburb and ended up back in Cleveland at about 152nd Street. After the WWII, taxes were so high that many of the properties lay idle and fell into serious states of deterioration. I do not know how that situation has changed. It may be that the City of Cleveland has taken over the area and now maintains the area (or fails to maintain it) much like it does the rest of the City of Cleveland.

The City of Cleveland has several landmarks that make it rather unique in many ways. For one, the Cleveland Terminal Tower complex constructed by the Van Swearingen brothers in about 1932 is still one of the famous buildings. All railroad passenger traffic used to come through the complex several stories below the street level. It is the terminus of the Rapid Transit which connects downtown Cleveland with Shaker Heights and points west of downtown to the airport.

Another waterway is the Rocky River that is located on the west side of downtown Cleveland separating the industrial area from the "nicer" residential areas in West Cleveland.

A monument to all veterans of wars is prominently located on the square of this county seat in front of the Terminal Tower complex. It is a very impressive monument. On the lakefront at about East 6th Street was located the old Cleveland Stadium which was constructed in 1931 and used for the World's Fair of about 1938. It was the home of the Cleveland Indians for the last 50 or so years. It was also used for the Cleveland Rams football team until 1946 when the Rams moved to Los Angeles and the Cleveland Browns football team from 1946 to 1995 when Jacob's field was finished. The Cleveland Indians moved from League Park sometime in the early forties after League Park had to be retired because of lack of maintenance and because the location was not suitable to handle large crowds. The Stadium could seat upwards of 79,000 people while League Park, as I recall, could only handle about 15,000 or less. Jacob's field was constructed for the Indians to provide a facility that had "modern" facilities for private boxes, etc. The Cleveland Stadium was taken apart and removed from the site in about 1998. The site has been used for other forms of public use.

Cleveland is different than any city in which I have lived. The industrial area of Cleveland, for many years, was a cesspool of pollution caused by the steel mills and the petro-chemical industries operation. In the early 1960's the State of Ohio passed serious legislation to control water and air pollutants. This occurred about the time the Cuyahoga River had the reputation of being the only river in the USA that could burn. This area which has made an impact on the City, is the area called "The Flats" located on the banks of the Cuyahoga River. The steel industry built up here along with the petro-chemical and other chemical industries. The Flats are also an area where many old abandoned factory structures have been converted to restaurants and other entertainment facilities.

There are many parks in Cleveland located in a strip of land around the City identified as the "Greenbelt". Gordon Park is the park closest to my early home and mentioned in other places of this writing. At this writing the park may well have disappeared because of the development of the interstate highway system along the edge of Lake Erie from downtown Cleveland eastward.

FAMOUS PEOPLE AND FACTS ABOUT CLEVELAND, CUYAHOGA COUNTY, OHIO

When I recall the "famous" people from Cleveland, I immediately remember Jessie Owens, a graduate of East Tech High School (where I also attended), and Olympic Medalist of 1936 in Germany. To my knowledge, he was the first black graduate who achieved national prominence as a 100-yard runner and long jumper. Another outstanding graduate was Harrison Dillard who followed Owens in the same competitions. These two black athletes brought much notoriety for East Tech H.S. and its graduates. Another East Tech graduate of some fame was Jim "Jughead" Martin. He played center for East Tech H.S., Notre Dame University, and the Detroit Lions professional football team.

Joseph Jurlina

During my senior year at Tech, the track team had 26 blacks and two white members. We often said that the black athletes developed their skills early in life while trying to outrun the police in their neighborhood that surrounded the High School located at 55th and Scovill Avenue. Only 65 per cent of the 3600-student population of East tech was white. As I mentioned previously admission to Tech was limited to about 400 freshmen each year determined by competitive examination - only the first 400 ranked were admitted.

East Technical High School was a vocational school for boys only, located in a predominantly black neighborhood only a few blocks from Central High School, an all-black non-vocational school. In addition to an all-vocational program East Tech offered college-prep courses which provided students with two years of a foreign language, two extra years of English, and two years of chemistry and physics in addition to the "standard" schedule of vocational classes. My vocational specialty was the "electrical" option that involved a study of basic motor/transformer design and repair, and residential/commercial wiring.

Cleveland was a typical melting pot of ethnic neighborhoods representing every area of Central Europe. In many families, the children in school studied English as their second language. Roman Catholics were by far the largest Christian group in the City. I cannot remember ever knowing a child that was not a "Roman Catholic". I never heard about Methodists, Presbyterians and Lutherans or that these were Christian denominations. I had never heard of a Baptist before my induction into the Army of the United States in 1943. In our neighborhood Jewish people were always referred to as "those Jews" and never accorded the status of normal people (how uninformed could a people be).

Most cities have a "Main Street" but as far as we were concerned, Cleveland had several such thoroughfares. We lived in an area that was between two Avenues, St. Clair and Superior. These two thoroughfares were unique to the east side of Cleveland running from about 6th Street east to beyond about 200th street, an area which I did not get into very often. In Cleveland, for the most part, the Avenues run from East to West and parallel to the shore of Lake Erie, while the Streets ran from North to South so that it was always relatively easy to keep track of your position in the City. Unfortunately, some of the suburbs that have contiguous boundaries did not all follow this convention. Since the city developed from the Lake-front toward the south, the newer and more desirable areas were several miles south of where we grew up. About the time I left home in March 1943, most of the people with the money to do so moved to the eastern and western suburbs to get away from our old commercial-industrial area.

The areas close to the lakefront, between St. Clair and Superior, were old ethnic neighborhoods that, as mentioned before, were clean and well maintained indicating that the residents were poor but proud of what they called home. The area south of Superior and north of Hough Avenue was the edge of a "pretty tough" neighborhood consisting mostly of blacks and other recent "white trash" arrivals to the city. Our neighborhood gave us children ready access to the Lakefront and the baseball field at Gordon Park that was about one mile from home. The people in our neighborhood were friendly as long as you stayed off their property. All the homes had fences of one kind or another around the entire properties. Whether that was for security or a carry over from Europe or utilized because the lots were all rather small I don't know.

We always had plenty to do outdoors during the spring, summer and fall months as long as the weather was mild enough to be outdoors. We played in the neighborhood, on the school playgrounds, in City parks along the Lake Erie water-front, along the railroad which separated our neighborhood from the Lakefront, or around the many factories which were located between the railroad and the Lake front. During the many inclement days of the year, not always in the winter, we went to the Cleveland Library located at 55th and St. Clair Avenue, not more then a mile away from home.

In the neighborhood we played "kick the can", bounced a rubber ball off the garage that was next door to our home and we played tag in and around the apartment house across the street from home. Of course, we played baseball and football in the East Madison school playground that is located about one block east of our house. We played tag on the fire escapes there also. Another form of entertainment in the playground was to scale the side of the school building to a window ledge made of sandstone that circled the building about 6-8 feet about the ground. We tried to circle the building on this ledge and more times than not we made it all the way around the building. During the summer months we played baseball in the city park and the playground until we almost dropped.

The City of Cleveland changed as we were growing up but I did not realize how much change was taking place. Our neighbors, that could afford to move, did so as soon as they could -- some before the war but mostly immediately after WWII.

MY RECOLLECTIONS ABOUT THE "GREAT DEPRESSION"

The "great depression" started about the time I was five years old which means that all the time I was in elementary school we were deep in the depression. I can remember that we never had much to eat but we always had something to eat that mostly consisted of soup or beef organ meats especially liver, heart and kidneys. Mother's kidney stew was one of my favorites but the preparation was always accompanied with odors that were not always pleasant and easy to avoid but the results were always "laripin". We always ate all that was available.

One incident about the depression and parochial school is very vivid in my memory. During grade school days our book bill for a year was about two to three dollars and always due before final grades were issued. One year, probably in the third grade, I recall the Rector of our Church came to present our report cards when my teacher, a sister of Notre Dame, told the Rector that even though I wore "new clothes" each day of the year I had not paid my book bill. What she obviously did not know or care to know was that I had one shirt and one pair of pants which my mother washed and ironed every night of the school year. I recall feeling injured not because of my embarrassment, but because she did not know of my mother's plight and determination and effort to keep us presentable in class in spite of our limited wardrobe. Nobody at the Church School seemed to know, although they should have guessed, that practically all the laymen in the parish were unskilled laborers and as such most were either unemployed, working few hours, and/or working for very small wages. That was certainly my father's situation in that I can remember him saying that at one time he was making 8-9 dollars a week at best and his mortgage payments alone were $20 per month.

The word "depression" brings back many more memories about how our family survived and how relatives and friends dealt with this rather tragic time. In our family, we did many things to reduce our "operating costs". For example, as we wore out the soles of our shoes my father replaced them with soles made from a synthetic rubber material that could be glued onto the old sole. Old heels were pulled off and replaced. It seemed that replacements were made with great frequency and until the shoe sizes were no longer adequate. Only then were new shoes purchased. Hand-me-down shoes were the order of the day; therefore, the oldest child (me in our family) was the only one who could expect to see a new pair of shoes every now and then.

Most of our Aunts and Uncles managed to apply for and received free supplies of staples from the Federal Government. I can also recall that my father would not accept this government handout because he was too proud. My father refused to lower himself to asking for, much less receiving, handouts of commodities such as butter, flour, etc. made at distribution centers around town; he didn't want to be beholden to any politician or government person because he felt there would be too many strings attached. He purchased his groceries and clothing on credit from those that would grant him such credit extensions. He paid those bills off as he could when the depression began to ease off and mother starting working in the defense industry. I can remember wondering at the time, "How will all this be paid for? Who has made all this possible?" Taxes meant nothing to me at the time but I am certain that the government largess that started back in the thirties has brought us to the point where people expect to be taken care of without any thought about who pays the bill.

The principal source of entertainment in those days was to have family gatherings at which little food was generally available, but much conversation about every conceivable subject was heard. In addition, it was during these gatherings that many tales about the "old country" and the "good old days" were heard. It was interesting to see how long a conversation would last over only one glass of homemade wine, beer or whiskey. Remember we had five Aunts and Uncles by marriage so there was much resource material with which to work. It is unfortunate that tape recorders were not available to record those conversations and tale telling. They would have been full of priceless information and probably a stretched fact or two.

Mother supplemented our family income by doing laundry for her sisters and their husbands. Most of this activity happened as the depression was winding down and the relatives were mostly back to work, but none-the-less it was important as income. I can recall so many days, particularly during the winter months, when mother would wash four or five washer-loads of clothes after the youngest children were in bed and then she would try to iron those clothes before morning. Washing clothes in the old Maytag washer was a "great" experience too because the wringer (this was before the advent of spin-dry cycles) 90% of the time was broken and the clothes had to be partially wrung out by hand and then hung up to dry in our basement. I helped all I could and probably complained while I was helping. It really distressed me that my mother had to work 18-20 hours a day for as long as I could remember without having any apparent hope for times of recreation.

When I was about twelve years old in 1936, movies were available for five cents or a dime at the Norwood Theater and it was very exciting to be able to go on occasion. I am not sure whether it was the attraction of the movies or the door prizes and gifts given on entry that attracted us. I can remember the pink and green depression-glass pieces that were given to all ticket holders on special occasions. I know that mother appreciated having them and looked forward to our bringing them home, but she never to my knowledge attended a movie while I was living at home until March 1943. My mother's principal entertainment came from reading anything she could get her hands on, including The Cleveland Press, Saturday Evening Post, and other magazines for which I sold subscriptions and managed to get extra or back issues. Mom's sisters also kept her supplied with reading material of various kinds. Movie going must have been a great form of reality escape for the adults that went to the movies but neither of our parents attended movies.

CITY BOY

Movie stars of the era, for the most part, lived in the fast lane with much more money than the average citizen. Many of the California-based stars seemed to be out of touch with the reality of living in a real world and tried to make real the fanciful roles many of them portrayed on the screen. There were many fairly decent-role models and probably many more that we did not hear about. The newspapers and radio personalities talked more about the "fast-livers" than they did about the sensible and sane.

During the depression, all holidays were celebrated but in a very subdued fashion and at home with minimal special foods or gifts because of the scarcity of money. Most holidays were celebrated by having gatherings of relatives who surely brought dishes to add to our own, as our family surely did not have the rations for large crowds. I remember the long discussions about incidents that had occurred in the lives of all the adults present. There were many stories I wish had been recorded for all of posterity to hear about the good and the bad times adults related.

I was too young to know the exact causes of the great depression but I did recall some adults talking about how some of the "big money" people were buying stock without putting up much of their money. As a result, when the bottom fell out and they were called upon to clear up their debt, they had nothing to fall back upon and had to liquidate at a time when not many people had money to take advantage of the bargains available. Those that had liquid assets did very good and those that didn't just did without. Many committed suicide in their desperation.

President Herbert Hoover's policies might have been effective had they been given more of a chance to work. President Franklin Delano Roosevelt took some radical steps to get the economy moving, in my mind at least; however, the economy did not respond until the war or near-war situation that was working in Europe as a result of Adolf Hitler's policies in Germany. The country took several giant steps toward a socialistic system with the strong personality of Roosevelt in power.

When Franklin Delano Roosevelt took office in 1932, I was only eight but I can remember that everybody in my family and neighborhood thought that he would be the savior of our world. One of my uncles worked as a precinct worker or some such responsibility. I can remember him having us pass out literature for Roosevelt and a Democrat candidate for Mayor by the name of Miller

Before the crash of the stock market there was plenty of optimism about our economy, in fact, over optimism is what created problems. Optimism did not return until we defeated the axis powers in Europe and the Japanese in the south Pacific. The advent of solid-state circuitry changed the USA and the rest of the world. Technical creation in addition to the rebuilding of Germany and Japan created markets for the new products being produced.

Another aspect of the depression era, say from 1919 till 1933, was the Prohibition Era, a period during which the manufacture and sale of alcohol for consumption was illegal under the 18th Amendment. I never researched this era much since I was only nine years old when the Amendment was repealed in 1933. It was in this time frame when my father and his friend from Croatia cooked up a plan to go into the business of making whiskey for sale to their friends. Under this arrangement, my father was to make the whiskey in his basement and his friend was to handle the sale of the whiskey. As I recall my father brewed up 2-3 different batches of the stuff and I helped to caramelize the sugar used to give color to the whiskey. By the time the last batch was prepared my father's friend had not given him any money for the whiskey which had been sold. I believe the story told to Pop was that he would get his money after this last shipment. Apparently Pop never received any money and the last time I saw this "friend" my father chased him off our property and in his hand he had one of mother's largest knives. Fortunately, Pop did not catch up with him. That was the last time I ever saw our "friend" in our home.

WHAT I REMEMBER ABOUT POLITICS AND THE DEPRESSION DURING MY YOUTH

President Roosevelt's first "fireside chat" took place in March 1933; I had just turned eight in September 1932. I do not recall what he said although I remember my Aunts and Uncles talking about how Roosevelt was going

CITY BOY

to save the USA from disaster. Looking back on the events that took place it was more like the first large step toward Socialism - taking from the haves in the form of taxes and redistributing it to the poor. As a temporary measure it would have been OK but unfortunately, it turned out to be more permanent rather than temporary because we have been living with that philosophy for a long time since.

The first hundred days in office for Roosevelt's administration are remembered because of all the "fixit" programs that were instituted, and as mentioned earlier, they were conceived to get the idle back to work and restoring confidence in the people that tomorrow would be better. From recollections there was little change in the employment picture until preparations for war began. One of the projects undertaken was to reform the banking system in an attempt to restore confidence in the banks. That move must have meant a lot to those that had any money to bank - we certainly were not in that class.

Another act written by Roosevelt and enacted by Congress was the National Recovery Act or NRA as it was called. This act granted businesses the right to set prices and control production levels which action contradicted existing anti-trust laws. Ultimately, it was declared unconstitutional and void, but the only thing I can recall was that the posters that advertised the NRA and appeared in all commercial and industrial establishments were a composite of red letters, white background, and a black eagle with its wings spread out. It looked rather ominous to me and reminded me of the German Swastikas which were seen all over Germany and shown in the movie newsreels. Again, this action may have helped the economy but the conflict with the constitution and existing laws made the whole process seem rather radical.

Unions gained popularity during Roosevelt's New Deal administrations, a fact that I can attest to because many of my mother's family members talked about the Unions. My father could not stand the thought of paying someone tribute to keep your job so he was rather vehemently and vocally opposed to the Unions. A good reason for his opposition was the fact that he was making a small wage, just barely enough to feed his family, and the thought of having to give up a pretty significant part of his wage to pay tribute to some shyster Union Boss did not sit well with him. He was an excellent judge of character and he saw through the "honesty of concern" of his Union representatives. In his case neither wages nor working conditions improved because of the Union activity.

The Social Security System was created about 1935 ostensibly to provide income for wage earners after retirement. I will never understand why Congress and all the financial brains of the country did not design a forced savings program for all wage earners that would take small amounts of wages, comparable to the S.S.S. deductions, and invest it in the companies of America, rather than the program which was enacted. I suppose looking at this program in retrospect is easier than it was at the time for the people involved in the process. What really worries me now though is that we have had about 60 plus years experience with a program that needs fixing and we have not fixed it yet and more pathetically, we have not admitted it needs fxing.

Our Jurlina family suffered through the depression in a very sad state and stayed there until after WW II started and I was graduated from East Technical High School in June 1942. Shortly after my graduation, my mother started working for the Fisher Body Division of General Motors Corporation where she worked on sewing the upholstery together for seats in GM cars made in Cleveland. She worked at this job all during the War - I am not certain when she retired from that occupation.

I believe that the USA economy would have recovered fully without Roosevelt's New Deal because of the War in Europe alone. I do not know whether any economists would agree with that belief. On the other hand, the War in Europe was a result in part of the depression in Europe also, so it is a matter of which came first. The depression made a significant impression on my peers and me. It taught us that life was hard and each person has the responsibility to provide for himself and his family. Relying on others to provide sustenance was risky and bad because when trouble hits it generally affects the entire community and not just one family. With the community in trouble there is no relief to be had for all those in need; therefore, the adage "the Lord takes care of those who take care of themselves" seems applicable - or said another way "be prepared" or "always ready", etc.

CITY BOY

WILSON AVENUE JUNIOR HIGH SCHOOL & EAST TECHNICAL HIGH SCHOOL

Wilson Avenue Junior High School was the public school that served the ninth grade students who came out of the eight-grade of parochial and pubic schools in the area. I think the school was located on Wilson Avenue just east of 55th Street between St. Clair and Superior Avenues. It must have been just east of the Wilson Avenue Methodist Church on 55th Street.

The school had classes from grades seven through nine. It was a relatively new public school building compared to the parochial school we had just left. It was a coed school that was not a new experience for us; however, the teachers were all civilians (not nuns) and that was a little strange at first. Some of the teachers were excellent and supportive of the children from parochial schools - I believe we were better behaved and better students scholastically.

One teacher who always comes back to mind when I reflect on my time at Wilson Avenue Jr. H. S. is Miss Chorpening. She was my English teacher and the one responsible for almost failing me because she could not read my writing. In self-defense I started printing everything in her class and all the others - remarkably, all my grades improved. Another problem she had was tragic but comical, especially to teenagers. When she started to explain anything or when she was correcting a student personally if she stared at the student for a few seconds her eyes crossed. It was a very scary event and something over which she had no control. Needless to say, some students were not very charitable in their reactions to this situation - which made matters worse for all. I thought I was one of the better students in all classes except English, again because my teacher could not read my writing for the first half of the semester. My decision to print instead of using cursive writing made a great difference but my teacher never warmed up to me. I am not sure if I was an exception to the rule or not!

None of the other teachers or subjects made much of an impression on me. I guess the change in environment from St. Vitus to Wilson was more traumatic than I realized. I suppose that all the St. Vitus "graduates" had much the same experience - we were generally placed in the same classes at Wilson Junior High. No special uniforms here (or at St. Vitus) were required at that time; however, my mother made certain that my pants and shirts were freshly washed and ironed. This meant that she laundered our school clothing every day. To that extent we were very well groomed. Hairstyles were not a factor except that boy's hair was always kept short to preclude the problem with hair lice, etc.

We graduated from Wilson Avenue Junior High School without any fanfare or special recognition - we were simply moved from the ninth grade to the 10th grade at High Schools across the City of Cleveland. Some students went back to Roman Catholic High Schools

CITY BOY

while many went to High Schools close to their homes. Al Vidmar and all my buddies and I from St. Vitus took the entrance exams required for us to attend East Technical High School located at 55th and Scovill Avenue deep in the heart of a black neighborhood. The area around the school developed early in the growth of Cleveland and had some very nice homes close to the school; however, as the neighborhood aged, many blacks moved into the area and it became known as the "Harlem" of Cleveland. Not a desirable area for poor white or any non-black folks. East Tech was a vocational school for boys only - over 3000 as I recall.

Admission to East Tech was limited to the 400 students with the highest grades on the admission test. Since the school was primarily a vocational school most of the students were concerned about getting training in one of the many trade courses offered. However, the school also offered a "college prep" option which could be taken along with the regular trade course. The basic difference with this option required the student to take an extra course of English, Mathematics, and two years of a foreign language. I opted for French but for some reason I could only take French for one year. It may have been that my working in the auditorium as an usher and part-time

JOSEPH JURLINA'S H.S. GRADUATION PICTURE - JUNE 1942

projectionist during lunch hours was a substitute for French. Our French Teacher was a "dapper" gentleman by the name of Mr. Giuseppe Cherubini who was a fine teacher as long as you behaved yourself. When we misbehaved or were not paying attention he would throw an eraser at the offending part or cuss us out in Portuguese. He taught several languages at other local colleges in Cleveland in addition to his teaching at East Tech.

An interesting procedure was developed at East Tech when dealing with boys that were wont to fight at school. Generally, any fighting on school property ended up with the offending two-some to be sent to the gymnasium where they were given 16-ounce boxing gloves and given the opportunity to resolve there issue in a boxing ring. Normally that did not take too many minutes to resolve almost any argument, that is, they get too tired to hold their gloved-hands up. If you managed to get into trouble by arguing with the teachers or general misbehavior you ended up in the principal's office for a paddling with a large flat paddle. The threat of a paddling was enough to keep order.

Graduation from East Technical High School was a rather big disappointing situation as I recall. If I haven't mentioned this elsewhere I should say something positive about graduation. Some 400 plus students were gathered at Severance Hall in East Cleveland for the very short service. We sang one song "The Lost Chord:" after which we received our diplomas, we then departed without much fanfare. The best part of this experience my mother insisted I wear a brand new suit. As it turned out it was the only suit I had when I was discharged from the Army in 1946. My wife did not recognize me in civilian clothes.

TEENAGE FRIENDS AND ACTIVITIES

Friends during my teenage years were for the most part those boys with whom I attended class at Saint Vitus; however, about a third of my classmates were new to me. That in itself was a bit traumatic because two of my lab partners in my Electrical Course Option, for the last semester, were black boys whose family economic status was much better than ours. A fact, that came as a big surprise to say the least, and one that changed my somewhat "warped" and parochial opinion about blacks. Hopefully, this respect for the other fellow has stayed with me through the years. I don't recall any conversation at home or in school about discrimination so we went about our business pretty normal for a bunch of Hunkies.

My really close friends all were from the neighborhood - in that day and time your close friends were those you saw and played with close to home because the only transportation we had was our feet; therefore, we played close to home. For the most part, we "hung out" in the Public School grounds of East Madison School located on 65th Street at Carl Avenue. Later in life, about January 1950, we lived across the street from the school on Carl Avenue in the home once owned by the Krall family.

A typical day at the playground for us was baseball, football or tag depending on the number of kids available and the time of year. Baseball for us took two forms. The first was a game we played with a red rubberball about the same size as a regular hardball used by the professional teams. A second form was one in which we used a "softball" which was either 12" or 14" in circumference and which were generally supplied by the City Recreation Department. In the fall, we played football with a ball that belonged to the boy with the "best" toys, ha! Again, these games were played at East Madison Elementary School.

Early in life TAG was a special form of a tag game that we played on the sandstone ledge of the school buildings. The stone ledge was about 6-8 feet above the ground depending on the location around the buildings. In order to stay on the ledge, which was no more than six inches long but at a 45 degree angle you had to hang onto the window sills where there was a sill, but in between windows where there was no sill you had to hold onto the space between courses of brick. About a third of the time you were between windows you usually fell off which meant you were inherited the "it" condition from whoever was in possession of the title at the time. Of course, the person who was "it" could get rid of the title by tagging the fellow in front of him or by having someone fall off the ledge.

We always managed to get in trouble with one of the immediate neighbors on the west side of the school. When we hit a baseball over the 10' chain-link fence between his home and the school the ball invariably ended up in his garden. If the homeowner was home, we could count on his coming out of his home to retrieve the ball before we could. If he got the ball first he usually complained about our hitting the ball into his garden and kept the ball. So, it was always a race to see how fast we could scamper over the fence, get the ball and then scamper back over the fence without being caught by the heels midway up the fence. Because of his attitude, it was not unusual for many of the boys to scale the fence and steal carrots or radishes just to antagonize the owner. I cannot imagine why we weren't shot at while in this mode of stirring up trouble. I have scars on more than one finger after hanging a finger on the barbs on top of the fence. We all played the game of "fence-jumping". When we were not in the playground we played "kick-the-can" or a form of "hockey" with a can in the middle of 63rd Street in front of our home.

THE 63RD STREET GANG AT EAST MADISON PLAYGROUND– ABOUT 1940
Dick Gerbec, Al Vidmar, Walter --, "Tarzan"
John Pinka, Eddie Baron, Frank Popotnik, Bob Yarshen
Brown

When I was about ten years old we had a neighbor who owned a bicycle and was in the habit of carrying another friend "double" on the handlebars. One day they were on their way to Gordon Park where we were to play a game of baseball on a park diamond. The boys headed for the park on the bicycle on 65th Street and as they crossed St. Clair Avenue on which there was an Electric Streetcar Line. The boys tried to beat the Streetcar at the intersection and lost - both boys died instantly as the car ran over them. This was the most devastating event in our lives to that point.

Although my friends and I had disagreements over minor matters, such as when we decided who would play on which team in our sandlot games; however, it never deteriorated into physical fights but more a war of words. One day during the winter, Al Vidmar was horsing around and snatched the knit cap I was wearing from my head and continued to taunt me by coming close to me and waving it my face. Finally, after several taunts, I managed to overtake him and was about to snatch the cap back when he fell to his knees during my charge. As a result, I stumbled over him and fell face forward into the curb of the street. I did not recall what happened for several days because of the concussion I suffered by the blow. I can remember that I was nauseated for several days and could not keep food down. Of course, I was left to recover by resting with no activity or school attendance without any medical attention. In those days, doctors were called or required only when you were unconscious. Whether some of my mental deficiencies can be traced to that incident is still open for discussion. If an autopsy is done at

ALBERT JAMES VIDMAR & JOSEPH JURLINA ABT FALL 1942

my death please have them look at the front of my brain to determine if any damage is obvious which might explain some of my strange actions during my life.

My friends were a very competitive bunch of guys when it came to sports only. They did not seem to care about competing in academics or for the attention of girls. The girls, however, were very competitive in academics and could not stomach having a boy win out with the best grades. Of course, you must remember that this competition only lasted through the eight-grade at St. Vitus Roman Catholic School. Things changed somewhat in the ninth grade at Wilson Avenue J.H.S. where we had some "older" girls to contend with. At East Technical H.S., vocational school for boys only, the competition got a little heavier and Al Vidmar, Jim Brown and Ted Chichocki led the pack of "high-graders"- I was down in the upper 10% group rather than the 1% group of 400 or so students in our graduation class. I tried to contact Ted in 2009 but could not find him.

Among my male childhood friends I suppose Al Vidmar was a very special friend since we were classmates for almost twelve years all the way through High School. I lost touch with him and all my other friends in March 1943 when I left home to enter military service in the Army of The United States. It is unusual that only one of my childhood friends, Henry Zabukovic and I ended up in the same outfit for Basic Infantry training at Camp Joseph T. Robinson located in North Little Rock, Arkansas. He did not stay at the Camp for long because he became very reclusive, and would not come out for training formations or food. He was granted a medical discharge as unfit for service. In some respects he was smarter than many GI's who stayed for training but died in action in Europe or in the South Pacific. I was fortunate because I ended up missing action in combat zones and served all my time in training situations and outfits. I have not seen Henry since we met at Camp Robinson shortly after we arrived there.

Teenage years are difficult years, as any adult will attest, and we had some tough growing up years. If it had not been for one or two close friends I couldn't have survived. They included Albert James Anthony Vidmar and John Misic. John was a couple of years older than I but he served as a listening post many times. Albert Vidmar received a BSEE

CITY BOY

from Case Institute in Cleveland after his wartime service. Albert died in 1988 with cancer just a month before the 50th reunion our 8th grade class. John Misic served in the Marine Corps in the South Pacific, retired as a Vice-President in Charge of Operations with the Cleveland Electric Illuminating Company and now (2010 retired) lives in Solon, Ohio.

Among my female childhood friends only one comes to mind as a close friend. That was Ruth Dulzer, the only daughter in a German family in which there were two sons, one a married civilian with family, and the other an ordained Roman Catholic Priest. I met Ruth while she was a cashier early in 1943 at the local movie theater on about 65th and Superior Avenue. On our first date she confessed to me she had plans to enter the Convent of Ursuline Nuns as soon as she graduated from a Roman Catholic High School she attended. I spent the next 60 or 90 days, just before leaving for the Army, trying to talk her out of doing such a "foolish" thing with her life. As it turned out she did not leave for the Convent until sometime in 1944 while I was stationed in Denton in the Army Specialized Training Program - apparently there was a serious illness in her family that delayed her trip to the Convent. She ended up as President of Ursuline College in the Cleveland, Ohio area.

I did not have a chance to vote until I was discharged from the service in February 1946. We lived in Throckmorton with Billie's parents until I could get a job. During a local election, Thomas Boyd, husband of my sister-in-law Louise, ran for the office of County Commissioner in his and our District. I voted for Thomas and he won by one or two votes (including Billie's and my vote) and his opponent challenged our votes. After a nasty court scene the County Judge finally ruled that a veteran could vote anywhere he called home and Throckmorton County was our home at that time.

President Reagan was one of my favorite politicians. He wanted as little government as possible and I agreed with his philosophy about that and the need for personal responsibility for one's life. It is unfortunate that he could not serve several more terms in office, because I felt he could have had a much more positive influence on the attitudes of our young people. It was obvious that he was a real "statesman" first and a politician last as compared to a majority of our elected officials since.

Joseph Jurlina

JOHN AARON GRABLE, BEALAH LOW LEE GRABLE, THOMAS E. BOYD
BILLIE GRABLE JURLINA, JOHN FRANCIS GRABLE, WILLIE VICK GRABLE, LOUISE GRABLE BOYD
JOSEPH JURLINA, JOHN R. GRABLE, BOBBY GLEN BOYD, THOMAS E. BOYD, JERRY LEE GRABLE
SUMMER 1945 @GRABLE HOME IN THROCKMORTON, TX

TRAVEL DURING MY TEENAGE YEARS

There is not much to say about travel in my teenage years for only one reason - we did not do much! I do remember one trip I took with Uncle Fritz Zerull and Uncle Bill Avenmarg. As I recall, we were in Uncle Fred's car and we drove east from Cleveland to a place on a running river and some lagoons to fish for some type of Bass fish. We did not stay long or we must not have driven too far because we were back in town much before dark that same day. I am not in a position to comment on how well the fishing went because I don' recall seeing any fish!

The second trip I can remember is one I took early in 1941. John Misic's father purchased a brand new Plymouth sedan for about $700 and John decided to drive to Detroit to see where the Tigers played baseball. We drove there and back the same day, a round-trip distance of at least 360 miles. I do not recall telling my parents or my siblings that we were on our way. When we arrived at Tiger Stadium we simply drove around the place and started back home without so much as a long look. A ballgame was in progress and there were many people on the streets around the stadium. By my present recollection, these are the only times I ever was taken out of town until I was drafted into the Army of the USA in 1943. I do not recall ever having slept anywhere else than in our home before I left for the service.

MY EMPLOYMENT AFTER HIGH SCHOOL

After graduation from high school in June 1942 I, along with my fellow graduates, looked for employment situations in the Cleveland area. Most of the industrial employment opportunities were in firms whose primary concerns revolved around the defense business. I decided early on that I should try getting employment with a firm that would be around after the war was over; therefore, I looked at the electric utility in Cleveland known as the Cleveland Electric Illuminating Company or CEICO. After a very short interview I was hired to start work in the meter department reading residential meters out of the Service Center located in the southeast part of Cleveland off Broadway Road. John J. Misic, a very good friend offered to be my main personal reference, had worked for CEI for a couple of years before he enlisted in the Marine Corps early in 1942. My salary was eighty five dollars ($85) per month. I should note here that many of our classmates were employed in defense plants and were making $85 per week including overtime work available. I should add that we were anticipating being called for military service very soon, but we hoped to return to work for CEI after the war.

In those days the meter readers were given a book, for the meters on the route to be read, which contained a history of readings for each meter. In addition to readings for each customer there was a line of instructions for each customer such as; *"Knock on the door and call out METERMAN to announce you presence. Proceed to the meter in the basement after you get a positive response."* In one such case, I knocked on the door, opened it and heard an OK and proceeded to the basement stairwell. After I had taken about two steps into the house I came upon a family of four seated at a table at mealtime.   The oldest female teenager at the table was furious that I had entered the home in such a crude manner and protested to her father that I had no right to be there at that time.

Joseph Jurlina

Fortunately, the father indicated with a nod that it was OK for me to proceed. It was obvious to me why CEI was in a program to remove indoor meters.

After reading meters for about six weeks I was moved into the meter testing group where we repaired old indoor meters (I-14 5 ampere) and prepared them for shipment to various Mexican and Central American utilities. This involved cleaning the meters, painting the bases, testing the meters and packaging them for shipment. The meters were ready for use in the CEI system; however, our indoor meters were being replaced with meters installed in outdoor locations, a program which had been in place for about three years before we were involved. I was involved in the meter repair business until February of 1943 when I received notice of my call to serve in the military.

THE WORLD SITUATION JUST BEFORE 7 DECEMBER 1941

As I recall, the German Armies under Adolf Hitler invaded Poland on 1 September 1939 and two days later France and England declared war on Germany. I was almost fifteen at the time and I recall wondering how that could happen just 21 years after the end of World War I. There were no reports that we heard that Poland had done anything to justify a war at this time. I do not recall any mention on the radio or in the newspapers of the events that led up to this action, and as a result, I was baffled how

CITY BOY

such an incident could occur with so little fanfare in the United States of America.

At this point I was not certain how France and England, our allies in WWI, could be involved in a war and not have the USA involved sooner or later. Of course, based on our horrible experience in WWI I also wondered how in the world anything like this could happen again. There was so much talk of our minding our own business by the isolationists at the time that I did not understand that either. I could not understand how Nazi Germany could expect to start another war without the rest of Europe and even the USA not having some great concern about the need to snuff out such an action by the Germans before it spread world-wide.

Then, when the Japanese bombed Pearl Harbor there was no doubt in my mind that we had the start of an international crisis and war that would involve every able-bodied person in the world. I remember I was sitting at my desk in my bedroom doing my high school homework and listening to the Boston Philharmonic Orchestra, when the program was interrupted for a special bulletin about the bombing at Pearl Harbor, Hawaii. The next thing we heard was President Franklin Roosevelt speaking to a called joint-session of Congress asking that a state of war be declared between the United States of America and the Empire of Japan. All of which confirmed my view that we would be in a war very soon.

AFTER THE START OF WWII

Sometime after the start of the war I learned that many Japanese-Americans from the west coast were interred in detention camps because there was a fear of sabotage by some of the people who were of Japanese extraction. I had never met any Japanese in my entire life (18 years) so I had no feelings about the Japanese-Americans one way or another. Based on my experience with other foreigners in our neighborhood I never met any persons about whom I was suspicious. My father was not a citizen at the time but I surely could vouch for him.

Because we declared war on Japan after the bombing of Pearl Harbor I knew for certain that was the reason for the war; however, in retrospect I do remember that the Japanese had been flexing their muscles against China and had made overtures toward others in the Far East.

My impression of Franklin Delano Roosevelt was that of a typical teenager. Having grown up in a family that was all Democrats I was prejudiced against Republicans by my environment. As I listened to him over the years, I found a man of an intellect greater than any of my larger family or teachers. Mr. Roosevelt seemed to have an answer for all the problems that confronted the USA at the time; therefore, I was impressed with his apparent ability to solve all the problems. Unfortunately, I was not a student of the Constitution and did not know some of what he proposed and had Congress enact was pretty much a series of socialistic schemes to put the Federal Government in control of all aspects of our lives. And if not downright socialistic, many proposals were unconstitutional. In spite of all that, he led the people with very positive, although very dangerous, recommendations that are a characteristic of good leadership.

"FDR" died on 25 April 1945 and Harry S. Truman, Vice President, became President. I knew very little about Mr. Truman and had no idea what kind of qualifications the man had other than he was Vice President. On that basis I thought that any man that could make it to be Vice President should be able to handle the job quite well. In retrospect he turned out to be the right man for the job.

On 6 August 1945, American planes, under orders from President Harry. S. Truman, Commander-In-Chief of US Military Forces, dropped an atomic bomb on Hiroshima, Japan and a second bomb was dropped on Nagasaki a few days later. This was done to force a quick end of the war with Japan. Most of the people I knew were very positive about the event since many had lost relatives in the Pearl Harbor disaster. At my tender age of 21, I thought it was the thing to do. Even at this writing, almost 65 years later, I believe it was the most practical thing to do to save much further loss of lives of our military forces and civilians in the Far East.

The fact that we had that kind of power did not make me feel safer since any country with educated physicists and engineers could do the same thing in time. In fact, German scientists under Adolf Hitler were working on a similar project to develop nuclear weapons. Not only that, but Germany was also about to introduce proto-type jet aircraft in Europe. These aircraft, along with nuclear weapons, could have changed the outcome of WWII and started a process of enslaving the world per Hitler's dream. During World War II, the Nazis systematically exterminated millions of Jews, political prisoners, Gypsies and others who were considered "enemies of the state". In my mind this was the most despicable, horrific unjustified act of murder that any sane person could imagine. I could not understand how any rational person could take part in such a process and I concluded that those responsible should be accorded nothing better than hanging or a firing squad. I could not understand how such brutal behavior could be conjured up in the mind of any sane person.

I did not know any person who had been a prisoner of war (POW) in an extermination camp; however, I knew of one P-38 pilot who was captured and imprisoned in a German POW camp near the town of Rothenburg on the Tauber River, Germany. The pilot was Carlton McAnear, a member of the TP&L Economic Development Group. Carlton related the following story about how he became a POW. He was returning to England after a photo reconnaissance-mission over southern Germany one spring day enjoying the sunshine at about 40,000 feet, and feeling rather safe and confident that no German aircraft could reach him from below at his altitude. It was not until he looked over his shoulder into the sun and saw two German planes diving down at him from a few hundred feet above his position did he discover how wrong he had been. Apparently they had taken a long time to get above him and just high enough and behind him that he did not notice them. They took advantage of their position and one pass at him during which they destroyed his hydraulic system before he could take evasive action. This forced him to land on the outskirts of the old walled-city of Rothenburg where he was taken prisoner and retained until the end of the war. He said he was more fortunate than many other pilots for his captors treated him according to the Rules of War of the Geneva Convention.

He told me that if he had seen the planes a few seconds earlier he could have out-climbed them easily and been out of reach in a very short time.

Furthermore, they would not have had the capability to reach him at the altitude his plane could reach. He guessed that the German pilots had been out trying to see what altitude they might reach with their aircraft when they saw him just below them. American intelligence had reported that their aircraft were not noted for achieving his cruising altitude and he felt safe. He considered this incident as an absolute fluke of events. Carlton McAnear died in 1977 while in open-heart surgery in Dallas, Texas.

My involvement in WWII was 34 months of my youth in the Army of the USA in the ETO theatre. Not in the European Theatre of Operations but the Theatre of Eastern Texas and Oklahoma. Therefore, I did not see any combat and much massive destruction except that which trainees can do while in basic and advanced training.

I left home in 1943 to serve in the U. S. Army and my brothers Tom and Bob left home also to serve in the army during the Korean War. My mother died in 1960 after a year of suffering with lung cancer so my father was left to live alone except for the years just before Bob married. Bob married Dorothy Thaler in November 1969 and they set up housekeeping in their own home in Brooklyn, Ohio a west side suburb of Cleveland. Dorothy died suddenly in February 1994 at the age of 65 years. After Bob's marriage, Pop lived alone. He died suddenly in 1979 at the age of almost eighty four while reading the paper on the living room sofa.

MILITARY SERVICE IN THE ARMY OF THE U.S.A. FOR JOSEPH JURLINA

My 18th birthday was on 19 September 1942; however, I was not called into the service until March 1943. Originally, I was scheduled to report for duty on 10 March 1943; however, for some reason, that I do not now recall, I did not report to the Cleveland, Ohio Induction Center until 17 March 1943.

To say I was looking forward to my time in service is an under statement because this new step in my career looked like a blessing in disguise. That is, I considered it a step forward and a way out of a life-style into which my siblings and I had been born. That deserves more explanation because I could not have been born into a family with more love for children and other extended family-members. My parents loved us more than life itself based on the sacrifices I saw them make for their children and relatives. From the time I was about nine years old until I left home for the military service, we experienced what has been referred to as the "great economic depression". And it was not until late in WWII or just after, before the country in general and our family, in particular, was in a position to look forward to the future with a positive attitude.

It was in this low period it seemed that my father and almost all of my male relatives by blood and marriage took to what I call serious drinking. The men mostly would start their weekends on Friday after 5 by going to the local bars, and sometimes at home, to eventually get "plastered". This condition generally continued until mid-day Sunday when the necessary drying-out period had to start so that they could make it to work on Monday. During these periods, life for my mother and some other women in our extended family was absolutely miserable. In my mind, if some of the women could have afforded divorce proceedings they would have, in spite of the terrible stigma that was placed on "divorced couples". A few wives, who wanted their marriages to work out, come hell or high water, chose hell and joined their husbands in the bars. How this affected the children in families involved is open to discussion. At my age and experience, anything, even military service and the inherent dangers, looked like an improvement. As I look back on those days, I must thank God that I was born twenty years or more after my parents were and did not have to suffer through the period they did while raising families. It must have been akin to hell on earth. But back to my experiences in the military service during WWII.

Joseph Jurlina

Prepare in Duplicate

Local Board
Cuyahoga County
FEB 23 1943
4900 Euclid Ave.
Cleveland, Oh

February 23, 1943
(Date of mailing)

ORDER TO REPORT FOR INDUCTION

The President of the United States,

To **Joseph** — **Jurlina**
(First name) (Middle name) (Last name)

Order No. **11782**

GREETING:

Having submitted yourself to a local board composed of your neighbors for the purpose of determining your availability for training and service in the land or naval forces of the United States, you are hereby notified that you have now been selected for training and service therein.

You will, therefore, report to the local board named above at **Rm. 310, 4900 Euclid Bldg.**
(Place of reporting)

at **7:00 a.** m., on the **10th** day of **March**, 19**43.**

This local board will furnish transportation to an induction station. You will there be examined, and, if accepted for training and service, you will then be inducted into the land or naval forces.

Persons reporting to the induction station in some instances may be rejected for physical or other reasons. It is well to keep this in mind in arranging your affairs, to prevent any undue hardship if you are rejected at the induction station. If you are employed, you should advise your employer of this notice and of the possibility that you may not be accepted at the induction station. Your employer can then be prepared to replace you if you are accepted, or to continue your employment if you are rejected.

Willful failure to report promptly to this local board at the hour and on the day named in this notice is a violation of the Selective Training and Service Act of 1940, as amended, and subjects the violator to fine and imprisonment.

If you are so far removed from your own local board that reporting in compliance with this order will be a serious hardship and you desire to report to a local board in the area of which you are now located, go immediately to that local board and make written request for transfer of your delivery for induction, taking this order with you.

Member or clerk of the local board.

D. S. S. Form 150

CAMP PERRY, OHIO - OUR FIRST MILITARY STOP IN SERVICE

My first stop toward a "military career" came when we left Cleveland by bus and arrived at Camp Perry, Ohio a 2-3 hours later to be introduced to the Army of the United States. It was here that we were given; a medical examination, the shots required of new recruits, psychological tests to

CITY BOY

enable classification of us for various service areas, issues of GI clothing for winter and summer, and some military indoctrinations.

Camp Perry in March 1943 was a cold, wet and forbidding place to be introduced to the Army. As I recall, all the recruits there were from places in Ohio; however, it was a strange looking lot gathered outside every morning for about two days in line waiting for the next "military event" to take place. We had not yet been introduced to military formations at this place, for that was to happen in "basic training" somewhere else. We were just called out on the sidewalks in mobs and directed to the various tents for the next event. We must have looked like the dead-end kids and to those standing on the sidelines we must have looked like a pitiful lot. On the second cold morning we were served breakfast in our "new issue" metal mess-kits and cup. The food consisted of scrambled eggs and bacon with two pancakes and a liberal supply of honey or syrup ladled onto the "mess". Before we could get in a position to eat the food outdoors the conglomeration in our kit were so cold and congealed we could turn our mess-kits upside down and nothing would fall out. Later that day we lined up to get some of our shots. The young man in front of me passed out just as the man in front of him was getting his shots. On the morning of the third day at Camp Perry, we were told that a group of us were to ship out for our next stop to a basic training camp. Sure enough, about 250 of us boarded a train for a location that was a deep military secret.

CAMP JOSEPH T. ROBINSON IN N. LITTLE ROCK, ARKANSAS - OUR SECOND MILITARY POST

About 16 hours and two Red Cross meals later we arrived at the gate of Camp Joseph T. Robinson located north of Little Rock, Arkansas where we were assigned to rather new "huts" that were large enough for a platoon of about 40 men. As I now recall, basically the huts were large enough for double-bunks (lower and upper), a footlocker for each man, a two-foot horizontal bar per man for hanging our uniforms, two wooden-racks for rifles not yet issued, two small, pot-bellied stoves for heating the quarters, and finally a space for the Platoon Drill Sergeant about 10' by 10' comparably equipped for his personal and military equipment. The huts had wooden-sides about four-feet high above the floor and the rest of the walls were a fiber netting the rest of the way to the ceiling. On the outside of the huts canvas drop cloths were used to cover the netting. These canvas sheets could be rolled up or down and in the down-position during the rains and /or freezing temperatures.

North Little Rock was a very nice city before the US Army came along. There must have been 50,000 GI's stationed at Camp Robinson during our Infantry Training of March-June, 1943. On weekends when some soldiers had weekend-passes the streets were literally filled with military people making the city look more like a military base. The women of the city, according to military propaganda, were to be avoided like the plague because statistically 50 % of them had a venereal disease. This, to me, seemed absurd but I had no basis for argument. The natives were extremely friendly, and for the most part, treated us very well. The United Service Organization (USO) there was one of the best we ever experienced.

The basic training at Camp Robinson was pretty standard for Infantry personnel and consisted of about twelve-weeks of exposure to military law, physical training, military discipline, and many miles of marching.

CITY BOY

After the first month of training, and on a weekly basis afterward, we were exposed to long walks with full-field packs weighing about 30-40 pounds and M-1 Garand rifles weighing about 7-8 pounds. To start with our "walks" were only 8-10 miles round-trip; however, during our last eight or so weeks of training the walks lengthened to 25-30 miles and many cross-country treks through wooded areas. With one or two minor exceptions, these treks were taken in-stride by all. Fortunately, the weather was always pleasantly cool but on many occasions very rainy. In fact, during our stay there in 1943, the spring rains were so heavy and frequent that the Arkansas River, which runs through Little Rock, flooded the area and many soldiers from our base were called upon to fill sandbags and place them along the river bank to reduce the level of flooding.

It was at this location that I first met Glen Hansen, one of my best friends in the military. He and I were in the same platoon and housed in the same "hut" during our stay. Furthermore, he and I were 'upper and lower' bunk-mates for the period of training. Glen was born in Whitewood, South Dakota and when I asked him where that town was located, he said, "just north of Deadwood a few miles". Actually, it is about 25 miles northwest of Rapid City, SD. Glen grew up on a farm and milked cows twice a day during his growing up days. As a result, his forearm muscles were well developed and matched the muscular development of the rest of his body. I do not now recall the name of our Commanding Officer; nor can I recall the name of our Platoon Sergeant who was a bright young man of about 22 years of age.

The rest of our platoon and the entire company were made up of men from 18 to 35 years of age with various backgrounds. Many were just out of high school as I was, while a few were, obviously, men with some business background, and the rest, amounting to about 10% of the company, were illiterates who had to be given special reading and writing training in addition to the military training. I could not imagine that there could be so many men in our age-range who could not read or write, but when it came to being physical and involved in our infantry drills they all did well.

Our platoon was an exceptional one, in that, under the leadership of our Sergeant, we were very cooperative and interested in doing better than any other platoon in the company. The spirit was high and we made a point of enjoying whatever task was presented to us in whatever weather condition. Of course, there were times when the belly-aching got pretty bad but always taken in stride.

In the course of our training, in addition to the rifle, we were exposed to hand-grenades, rifle grenades, the 30-caliber machine gun, bayonet and hand-to hand training. Our company executive officer, a First Lieutenant, was a large man of Indian-descent from Oklahoma, who considered himself an outstanding hand-to hand expert. He was always eager to demonstrate his ability with us greenhorns. Among our Cadre of non-commissioned officers was a Corporal of Philippine descent, who was also a terrific hand-to hand fighter. On more than one occasion, for demonstration purposes, the officer challenged the Corporal to attack him with drawn knife. It was obvious that the Corporal could have won the struggle, if left to his own skill and ability; but the Corporal always lost. All in all, I believe the training we received built up our confidence as soldiers ready for combat situations. Fortunately, many others and I were never called upon to demonstrate our ability in combat situations.

I should also have mentioned that, as part of our experience at Camp Robinson, we were given a battery of psychological and intelligence tests, the results of which were never discussed with us. Within a few days of the completion of our basic training the rumor circulated that some of us would go on to advanced infantry training while others were to sent for some special training. Sure enough a day after the completion of our program about 40 of us were loaded on a train bound for a place of no name – top secret.

CAMP MAXEY LOCATED AT PARIS, TEXAS - MY THIRD MILITARY BASE

About 4 hours after starting out we ended up at Paris, Texas where we boarded a bus which took us directly to Camp Maxey about 10 miles north of Paris. This camp, named in honor of Samuel Bell Maxey, was designed as a POW camp for Japanese prisoners of war. Our quarters were comparable to those at Camp Robinson; however, one difference was that the horizontal ceiling joists at Maxey were only about 5 feet –3 inches above the floor. It was impossible for me to walk from end of the barracks to the other without bumping my head on the rafters 3-4 times – I guess I was a slow learner, ha! We were not told why we were there or what fate they had in store for us.

While there we had no specific duties except to stay out of trouble. At our age and temperament, keeping out of trouble was not in the cards for us, especially when we were told we would not get passes to go to Paris anytime we wanted. We would only have about 30 GI's on pass at one time so that it might take 7-10 days before we would be given passes. The resourcefulness of these young GI's was impressive – someone acquired a chain-link fence-cutting device and cut a hole in the fence on the backside of the property away from the main gate. Those of us who wanted to go to town simply dressed up in Class A uniforms and left through the "gate" and hitch-hiked a ride into town. Citizens of Paris were not too happy with the crowd of GI's that ended up in town but the camp administrators took no action about us. Obviously, the use of this camp as a reclassification center was very temporary as we found out one day and for a short time the camp was used to house prisoners of war.

NORTH TEXAS STATE TEACHER'S COLLEGE AT DENTON, TEXAS - MY FOURTH MILITARY POST

After about two weeks we heard that 500 of us were to leave by train for another secret post the next morning. It turned out that the lucky 500 ended up at Ohio State University in Columbus, Ohio and placed in a Army Specialized Training Program (ASTP) as pre-engineering students. Within a few hours after they left, 250 of us, including Glen Hansen and myself, were rounded up and told to be ready to leave in 2 hours. We boarded a train and left for a secret place obviously west of Paris and in about three hours more or less on July 4, 1943 ended up in downtown Denton, Texas about 40 miles north of Dallas. We disembarked with our duffle bags and loaded them on military trucks fully expecting we would also be given similar transportation to a place not yet divulged. That was a not to be, because after our bags left we were ordered into a company formation and started marching toward the west out of the station. It was only then that we were told we were headed for the campus of what was then North Texas State Teachers College about 1-2 miles away to enter an ASTP program of pre-engineering. In later years the school name was changed to North Texas University.

Denton was and still is the site of two centers of advanced educational institutions – North Texas State Teachers College as mentioned and another campus on the east side of Denton then called Texas State Women's College, now known as Texas Women's University. NTSTC had about 1,000 men and women registered while TSTC had about 600 women enrolled. From the standpoint of the lonely GI, nothing imaginable could beat such an assignment.

Meanwhile, back at the Denton Train Station, we were marched west to Avenue A on which were located about 10 co-op house of various sizes in which we were to be quartered. Glen and I ended up in Coke Hall, a small house in which about 15 of us were quartered again in double bunks. Glen and I were placed in the same room as bunkmates just as we were in Arkansas. Before 5 PM that evening we were introduced to our Company Commander 1st Lieutenant John McGiver and his Executive Officer 2nd Lieutenant McChesney (I believe his first name was Jonathan). We were given rules of behavior and schedule for the days to come.

John McGiver later in his life was a pretty successful actor in Hollywood and eventually on television as a character actor. I will admit his character acting was completely different than his military "acting". He died in 1975 as a result of a heart attack.

I failed to mention what the average military experience was of the 250 members of this ASTP Company. It turns out that about half of the Company were GI's of my caliber – that is, they had all just completed some simple infantry training. The other half, however, were combat veterans of the African Campaign and less than 20-30 days previously were killing Germans and Italians in Africa. Needless to say, many of this latter group were not the "student type" ready for the classroom experience we were all to face in a day or two.

CITY BOY

Our classroom schedules were rather hectic and, needless to say, strenuous because we were carrying the equivalent of 18-20 hours of course work. On Monday through Fridays our schedules started at 6:00 AM with a Reveille formation for attendance check, breakfast at 6:30 AM, formation for marching to class at 7:30 AM, classes from 8:00 AM till Noon. Our lunch served from noon till about 12:45 PM on campus, classes from 1:00 PM till 5:00 PM. Often during our time between classes we would lounge in front of the building in which our next class was to be held, and during these times a class of Home Economic students would walk by so I managed to beg for a sample of their cooking from a pretty young lady that later turned out to be my wife, Billie John Grable. I will expand on this later.

Our free time started after we got back to our quarters until 6:00 PM when we had dinner. From 7:00 PM till 10:00 PM was designated as compulsory study time in our quarters, lights out at 11:00 PM for sleep. The 11:00 PM "Bed-Check" was made at random times by a member of the non-com cadre acting as "charge-of-quarters". Violation of this study schedule resulted in the offender being cut from the program and returned to a replacement unit ready for return to combat. Needless to say, the rules were adhered to by most of the rookies such as Glen and me; however, the combat veterans enjoyed the challenge to violate the rules. As a result, many of the "old-timers" did little studying and failed the exams regularly and by the end of the first semester about 60 % of the original 250 flunked out and were replaced with new recruits.

As an aside, the NTSTC had a night guard who circulated around the campus to make certain the female students, who had a compulsory 10:00 PM check-in time at their dormitories were in their rooms - this gentlemen's name was Mr. Starr. You can imagine that, although the rules for the GI's and the women were specific and well advertised, both parties were want to break the rules for an occasional night out. All went well until Mr. Starr managed to identify the violators either on campus or in town. His batting average was not good but he always managed to find a serious offender, either male or female, and reported the violation to the proper authorities, civilian or military. I know of an incident where a ASTP student was followed by Mr. Starr to a point within a couple of hundred yards of the student's co-op house when the student broke and ran along through the backyards of the co-op houses in an attempt to shake Mr. Starr. In his hurry in total darkness, the student was making great progress running away until he encountered a low clothesline wire that struck him just below his chin. The blow knocked him down but he was able to recover and hide before Mr. Starr caught up with him. The student carried a swollen neck for several days before all evidence of the blow disappeared. Fortunately, Mr. Starr did not pursue the matter with our Company Commander and the student suffered no additional punishment.

According to the school records most of us amassed about 42 credits in College Algebra, Chemistry, English, Physics, American History, Texas History and Texas Government; however, when I registered as a freshman at the University of Texas at Austin, the Registrar, whose name I cannot now recall would not accept the bulk of my credits. Therefore, when I was a second semester Senior and had completed about 20 hours of advanced math, I was told I had to take College Algebra again. Needless to say that distressed me greatly, but no amount of pleading would change his mind. I firmly believe he was suffering from some type of dementia. After conferring with the course instructor I did not attend classes but took all the exams and the final exam and managed to get an A in the course. Although three hours was usually set aside for final exams I managed to complete my exam in about 20 minutes and as I turned in my paper and was exiting the room I noticed 2-3 freshmen look up and shake their heads. I do believe they suspected I had blown the exam and was leaving in disgust.

As I mentioned earlier, many members of our company were veterans of the African Campaign and very want to act as civilians rather than military personnel, so much so, that our Company Executive Officer, who was a portly gentleman, decided we needed to be given some extra physical experience such as a long march. So, one very hot July Saturday morning of 1943 we departed our Company area for a "long march" west on a country road of Denton. As is required in such military exercises, an Army ambulance followed our column. Our "great" leader, Lt. McChesney, took his position up front to lead us on this ridiculous mission. After about an hour or so into this trek, the temperature had risen to about 100 degrees; however, this gang of rowdy GI's sang songs and seemed to be enjoying themselves. We had not walked more than 3-4 miles when we noticed that the ambulance was moving forward to the head of the column. In another 3-4 minutes the ambulance returned and headed back to the campus with a patient aboard. It was not until we returned to our co-op houses three hours later that we discovered who the patient was – yes, it was our fearless leader Lt. McChesney. Needless to say, never again were we required to demonstrate our fitness.

Before we leave Denton, Texas I must say something about meeting my future wife, Billie John Grable, while on the campus of NTSTC. I may have mentioned this earlier in this treatise but, in the event I have not, Glen Hansen went to California to see his sister on one of his few days off and returned with a bottle of champagne. It must have been just after our Christmas break. Anyway Glen, Billie and I were enjoying the evening with a drink or two, just making small talk, when Glen excused himself and he disappeared. Well, there was nothing else to do but finish the champagne and make more small talk. Apparently, I had had too much of the sparkly and felt like I was getting sick so we just tried to get me well by walking off the effects of the drink. From that time on Billie and I saw much of each other without the presence of Glen to such an extent that we were developing a more serious relationship until, in about the first quarter of 1944. We were ordered out of Denton, after Congress in its great wisdom cut the funding for the A.S.T.P. program nation wide and we were to be transferred to a replacement outfit in Camp Howze located just outside Gainesville, Texas.

CAMP HOWZE - HOME OF THE 103RD INF. DIV. AT GAINESVILLE, TEXAS - MY FIFTH MILITARY LOCATION

Gainesville, Texas is just about 32 miles due north of Denton and Camp Howze was just outside the City limits of Gainesville. This was the home of the 103RD Inf. Div. in the Eight Service Command which was getting ready to deploy replacements in the European Theater.

Glen and I were assigned to a Heavy-Weapons Company with Glen getting into an 80mm mortar squad and ole Joe being assigned as a rifleman carrying a Browning Automatic-Rifle or B.A.R. as we referred to the weapon. We trained pretty hard for six or eight weeks until one day six of us in the Company were taken out of line and transferred by train back to Camp Joseph T. Robinson at N. Little Rock, Arkansas. I can only assume that the six of us were picked because we all wore glasses. The fact that we had been to A.S.T.P. in the pre-engineering educational program probably also figured in the move.

Unfortunately, Glen stayed at Camp Howze until the entire Division was deployed to Europe just in time for the "Battle of the Bulge" in the fall and winter of 1945. Glen was injured shortly after he arrived in the theater. It seems that in a forward movement of his Company, and during a barrage of our 155mm Howitzers, one Howitzer round dropped "short" and landed among Glen and his squad killing all of his men and wounding Glen very seriously. Glen lost his right arm at the shoulder and was seriously wounded with body wounds. After some treatment in a field hospital he was airlifted back to the States to the VA hospital in Temple, Texas where he stayed for months during his rehabilitation. After our separation at Camp Howze I did not hear from Glen until sometime after Christmas 1945 while he was recovering at the Veterans Hospital Temple, Texas. It wasn't until several years later on a visit to see Glen and his wife Margie in California that we heard the full story of how Glen lost his arm. It occurred one day while Glen and his mortar squad were awaiting orders about moving up toward the enemy line when a "short" American 155mm

CITY BOY

Howitzer round landed in the area where Glen and his men were standing. The blast killed all of his squad and blew his right arm off at the shoulder.

CAMP JOSEPH T. ROBINSON AT NORTH LITTLE ROCK, ARKANSAS - MY SIXTH MILITARY LOCATION

When we arrived at Camp Robinson, we were assigned to the 566th Field Artillery Battalion in "Charlie" Battery, a firing Battery of 105mm Howitzers. This really messed up the relationship between Billie and me by putting us about 200 more miles further apart.

The Field Artillery was more to my liking than the Infantry since we did not spend as much time walking or marching through the wilderness, but for the most part rode in some sort of vehicle from place to place. At least that was my early experience in "C" Battery. The six of us who first came to Camp Robinson were soon transferred into headquarters Battery. I can only assume that was done since we all had been in the A.S.T.P. and had enough mathematics to make us more valuable close to fire-control or surveying duties.

I met some really nice guys in this outfit, but unfortunately, I cannot now remember all the names. I did share a "hut" with a older Italian man from New York with the surname Buttafuco (spelling?). He was a barber in civilian life and so for the rest of my stay at Camp Robinson I had my hair cut once a week for the fabulous price of "four bits". Of course, each subsequent haircut amounted to a trim but the price was right.

It was while at Joseph T. Robinson this second time that I met 2nd Lt. Daniel J. Perrino on our HQ Battery Staff. For some reason he "took a shine to me' and one day asked me if I was interested in going to OCS, Officer's Candidate School. I agreed that would be an interesting move but I thought my near-sightedness (20/200) would prevent such an action. He then got a prescription from a pharmacist for some drops which constricted my pupils enough so that I could read the eye charts easily – this did not get by the committee and I was turned down as a candidate. I had no contact with Lt. Perrino after I was transferred to Fort Sill a new station near Lawton, Oklahoma until early in 2008, 64 years later, when I decided to look him up. I found two people in the Chicago area with the same name-spelling but the first number I dialed was his home phone in Urbana, Illinois.

We had what I thought was a remarkably interesting conversation reviewing our individual experiences since we last met. It was during this visit that he told me he was going blind with macular degeneration but otherwise in good health. He went on to relate to me his experience at the University of Illinois as a Professor of Music. It seems that in 1969, during the Korean War, and as was happening on other Campuses, many students were protesting the war and making a lot of noise on the campus. While he and a few of his contemporaries were having coffee in the Union Building on the "Quad" and discussing the noise of the students, someone mentioned that the disturbance was an unnecessary and unproductive activity and something should be done about the situation. Mr. Perrino thought that a "Jazz Band" would serve to redirect the attention of many. The idea caught on and the next day he and several of other faculty members brought their instruments to the Union Building at noon and started playing jazz as the first meeting of what later would be called "Medicare 5,7 or 9", The jazz band project was very effective in reducing the "noise" on the campus. In fact the group was active in playing "gigs" around the area from 1969 until 1998. Somewhere

JOE JURLINA, SPRING 1945 AT THROCKMORTON LAKE

in my files is a DVD which was made by TV Station W I L L to commemorate the successful project.

We weren't to stay at Camp Robinson very long because we were transferred to Fort Sill, Oklahoma after about 6-8 weeks, the exact time has long since eluded me.

FORT SILL, OKLAHOMA – HOME OF U.S. ARTILLERY - MY SEVENTH MILITARY LOCATION

Upon arrival at Fort Sill I was immediately assigned to the Surveying Group of the Fire Control Section in Headquarters Battery of the 664th Field Artillery Battalion. For some reason my stay in Surveying did not last very long and I was assigned to the Fire Control Section as a T-4 Sgt. having been promoted from Corporal along the way.

This location improved Billie and my situation since Fort Sill was only 75 miles from Wichita Falls, about 150 miles from the big city of Throckmorton and just a few miles from Lawton, Oklahoma. Therefore on occasion she and I could meet in Wichita Falls for a weekend.

It was at Ft. Sill that I was to meet Albert Bonney, Edward Mooradian, and Sgt. Jack Cruzen. These fellows made more of an impact on my memory than any others of the 150-200 that were in the 664th F.A.B. with whom I had much contact.

Albert Bonney was born in Virginia and later in life moved to Tampa, Florida area and then finally to the Stone Mountain, Georgia area. About seven or eight years ago he moved to Beach Bluff, TN which is about 15 miles from Jackson. He did this after his wife developed Alzheimer's disease and he wanted to be closer to his daughter who lives in the Jackson area. He is a man of many talents and a direct-speaking man. When I first met him he was a T-4 Sergeant. What I did not know was that he had just been "busted" from Staff Sergeant in the 664th. It seems that he was in charge of the non-coms in the fire control section and during a "shoot" by his Lieutenant, Bonney noticed that the officer's "initial sensing" (estimate of distance to the target) for the gun battery was way off but he decided not to say anything to the officer. It seems that

Bonney's opinion about the officer was not very high. As a result of the bad estimate the first shot from the howitzer destroyed some permanent property on the post. The Battalion Commander was so upset at the officer he had him transferred immediately, and when he finally found out that Bonney had let the mistake pass without comment, the Colonel told Bonney he could take a court martial or be lowered in rank one grade. Bonney chose to be lowered in rank. Not too much later I was given that Staff Sergeant's position but I did not know the history of Bonney's demotion until many years later.

Edward Mooradian, another good buddy of mine, was born in New York State near Troy and spent most of his life in the City of Troy near Albany. His family was in the retail furniture business for years and after his father passed away, Edward was the main cog in keeping the business going. He retired in 1986 at the age of about 63 and his younger brother has been operating the business since. While at Ft. Sill, Edward or "Mo" as we called him usually spent his free week-end time going to Paul's Valley, Oklahoma and another town, which I cannot at this writing remember, to visit a Methodist Church there and there just happened to be a college nearby on which campus there were many young female students. Of course, most of us yokels did not realize his reason for going there and "ribbed" him for making the trips. We have maintained contact with Edward through the years since leaving the Army. In 1987, when Billie and I were on a driving trip to Nova Scotia with the Lee Griffins, we stopped in Troy, NY to spend the night with Edward and his wife Doris. The Mooradians were very gracious and conducted a mini-tour of Troy for us before we continued on our way East. .

Just recently (2009) I called to see how he and Doris were getting along. It was then that I discovered he had had two very serious life changing events happen to him. The first was he was crossing the street in front of his home to mail a letter and was struck by a car driven by a young lady. He was hospitalized in intensive care for about a month and another month in a nursing home. He now had to walk with a cane to maintain his stability. The second happened more recently when he went to see his doctor about a sore throat only to discover he had developed cancer of the larynx. He has recovered fairly well after bouts of radiation and chemotherapy. His voice is a little more gravelly than before the treatments; however he is grateful for his recovery. Edward has had some serious problems of memory and hearing loss. He died early in the year 2009 after a long struggle with his throat problem.

Tech Sergeant Jack Cruzen was my roommate at the 664th at Ft. Sill and was our platoon sergeant. He was born in Iowa and was the only non-com in our outfit that owned an automobile – it was an old Buick, and as best as I can recall a 1937 or so model. He loaned it to me one week-end after Billie and I married so I could show her the countryside around Ft. Sill. It was a very pleasant experience to be free to drive around and not have to wait on public transportation. A few years ago when I was researching for my military friends I discovered that Jack had died some years earlier but I was not able to establish the cause of death.

It was while I was stationed at Fort Sill that Billie and I married on 12 May 1945 in Wichita Falls, Texas. Since I was an NCO I had access to live in Quarters for NCO's on the post. It was a very nice place, as military quarters for family go, and consisted of a living room, two bedrooms, a kitchen and one bath. I believe the rent was thirty dollars ($30) a month including utilities. As I recall now, some sixty-five years later, we purchased some furniture from a Sergeant who was just leaving the post. We were there for the remainder of our stay at Ft. Sill through early January when I was transferred to the separation center at Camp Atterbury near Indianapolis, Indiana to be Honorably Discharged "For the convenience of Government" on 2 February 1946.

Getting from Ft. Sill near Lawton, Oklahoma to Camp Atterbury was another experience to remember. While we were still in the uniform of the U.S. Army we were entitled to "bum" rides on military aircraft so about a half dozen of us went to Tinker Field near Oklahoma City, Oklahoma and hopped a ride on a B-17G which was being ferried to near Camp Atterbury. The pilot instructed us to ride in the bomb bay area and to stay out of the bombardier's place in the nose of the ship under the pilot's seat. We behaved ourselves most of the way but on the approach to the field in Indianapolis we stayed in the bombardier's area till we landed. Needless to say the pilot was furious but declined to say much.

Joseph Jurlina

BILLIE GRABLE & JOSEPH JURLINA IN DENTON, TX ABT FEB. 1944

CITY BOY

ADJUSTING TO CIVILIAN LIFE & FINDING A COLLEGE TO ATTEND

My Honorable Discharge from the Army of The United States was awarded to me at the Separation Center at Camp Atterbury, Indiana on 2 February 1946. The document lists me as Staff Sergeant in Headquarters Battery of the 664th Field Artillery Battalion in The Army of the United States with Serial Number 35052774. Along with this document I also

received a small amount of money I had coming such as back pay and some amount for travel to my home address in Cleveland, Ohio. I don't now recall the amount but it had to have been less than two hundred dollars. It wasn't until I left the base and started to hitch-hike to Cleveland that the realization struck me that I was now a civilian again and from that time forward I had to provide for my meals and shelter. It was a mixed blessing but I enjoyed the part where I did not have to worry about someone else telling me what to do and when to do IT!

As I recall the distance from Indianapolis to Fort Wayne, Indiana, the first leg of my "hitch-hiking" journey home, was about 130 miles. I started out from the Camp sometime shortly after lunch and when I was about 80 miles from Fort Wayne when I was picked up by a fellow driving a 1940/1941 Buick sedan. He was a mechanic at International Harvester on his way home in Fort Wayne. In an effort to make conversation, I commented to him how well the car was running. At that point he related how he had rebuilt the engine and this was his first trip home after the rebuild. He proceeded to show how well the car REALLY worked and proceeded to accelerate to somewhere between 70-80 mph with me white knuckled in the passenger seat. To make a long story short we made it to the center of Fort Wayne in just under an hour after he picked me up. Needless to say I was ready to get out of the car in one piece. The rest of the way to Cleveland, somewhere between 190-200 miles, was at a much slower pace and I did not get to 1157 East 63rd Street until just after dark. Thumbing a ride in those days (I was still wearing my uniform) was a good way to travel because to the average civilian the War was not yet over.

One of the first things I did the very next morning was to find out whether any of the old crowd was in town. It turned out that seven or eight of the East Madison schoolyard crowd were in town and had decided to play a game of "softball" in the East Madison School playground about mid-morning so I trotted out to get a pair of tennis shoes or some sort of footwear. It turned out that all I could find was a pair of spiked track shoes that must have been made before the war started so they must have been on the shelf for 8-9 years. I felt rather foolish wearing them but in the gravel field they felt better than street shoes would have felt. It was a great reunion for all concerned; however, we did discover that at least three of the "old crowd" had been killed and two seriously maimed while in action.

It was in the course of the conversation afterwards that the "Brown" kid and I had a discussion about how far it was from Cleveland to Chicago by road. He maintained that it was just over two hundred miles. He was very firm and argumentative about the matter and I knew that was in error so I challenged him to a bet. We settled on my $25 against his GI issue 45 caliber sidearm and holster plus about 500 rounds of ammunition. Apparently he had made off with the gun and ammunition while in the Navy. We checked the map and of course he lost, the distance is closer to 380 miles, so I ended up with gun and ammo. I tell this story only to relate another. While I was hitch-hiking home to Austin, Texas I had reached a point abut 100 miles from Cleveland when I was picked up by a business man in a long black Buick Sedan. He was in such a hurry to pick up this recently discharged GI (I was still in uniform) that he came out of his car to help me with my bags. As he picked up the one in which I had placed the gun and ammo he commented how heavy it was to which I replied that I was going to the University of Texas and had acquired a good many text books in Cleveland. He grunted and I said no more.

I returned to Austin via the road again hitch hiking the distance of about 1400 miles in a little over a day. Billie had preceded me and was staying with her Cousin Kathryn Brown, later to become Mrs. Kathryn Brown Howell, wife of Barney Lee Howell. In the months before this return to Austin we had discovered that all Campuses in Ohio and Texas had such an influx of Veterans who had applied for admission that none of the schools would accept a student's application to enroll unless the student had proof of having found a place to live. That was the reason for Billie going to Austin while I was in Cleveland – she was trying to find a place to live.

Joseph Jurlina

MARRIAGE WHILE IN SERVICE

As mentioned in earlier chapters of this treatise, Billie John Grable was a student at North Texas State Teachers College at the same time that Cadet Joseph Jurlina, Army of the United States, was a student in the Army Specialized Training Program (A.S.T.P. Unit 3890). That is, Billie started as a freshman in 1941 and by the time Joe arrived on the scene in 1943 she was well along in her studies going on to receive her Bachelor of Science Degree in Home Economics in August 1944. At that time Joe was a Private First Class in Camp Robinson located in North Little Rock, Arkansas, with a full four years of college ahead of him.

During our travel from one class to another we usually met girls who had been in a baking class in the school of Home Economics and Billie was one of the girls. I thought she was very pretty and usually made some remark about being hungry and would she bring a sample of her baking exercise for me to test. Needless to say she did that and it became a ritual of my asking for a sample each day. It was later in our stay that I met Billie through Glen Hansen and that story is detailed elsewhere in this discourse. Needless to say our relationship developed rather favorably in the near future.

With this background we should go back to establish when and how this relationship was established and who might have to accept some responsibility for the consequences. The relationship we are discussing is the marriage of Billie J. Grable and Joseph Jurlina which took place on 12 May 1945 in the First Methodist Church of Wichita Falls, Wichita County, Texas, with The Rev. Joe Z. Tower officiating. The ceremony took place at about 11:45 P.M. on the Saturday before Mothers Day. Why that late in the day is a story unto itself to be covered later. For those of you who might not know, The Rev. Joe Z. Tower was the father of John Tower, former U. S. Senator from Texas who served for two terms from about 1975 until 1987.

Our wedding was to be a surprise for my family back in Cleveland because I had not mentioned the possibility of it happening to my parents or any of my kin. Our rationale at the time was that because of the war, traveling would be quite a problem and the timing was such that they might not have a chance to make proper arrangements.

Back to the story about the late wedding service in Wichita falls, Wichita County, Texas, at the First Methodist Church. After Billie and I decided that the War was winding down and going our way and we should or could get married without too much fear of my having to go into a combat situation we set the date for 12 May 1945, at 8:00 pm. Unfortunately the two weeks before the wedding my unit was sent out on a two-week field problem during which we had no access to town or civilians so that I could not do anything about making any arrangements for us in town. A honeymoon was out of the question anyway for more than financial reasons because military "leaves" were not to be had at that time for people in our outfit.

When I got back to the Battery Headquarters that 12 May morning about 10:00 am we were told to get ready for an inspection of our equipment which had been out in the rain for most of two weeks. So we worked like crazy trying to get all of it cleaned up. After the inspection I told the Charge of Quarters (CQ) on duty that I just had to go to town for some last minute purchases and would be back post haste on the local bus. Meanwhile Billie, her sister Louise and her cousin Kathryn Brown, now Kathryn Brown (Howell), drove into Fort Sill looking for me. The CQ told them I had just gone into town, Lawton, on the bus. They decided to go into town to look for me. Of course, we passed each other on the way and it was not until several hours later that we finally got together and started to Wichita Falls about 75 miles from Fort Sill, Oklahoma. A much fuller recount of this is available anytime from my wife who can embellish this story with more details than I can now recall.

By the time we reached the First Methodist Church it was after 11:00 pm and so late that the organist had left the church and gone home to be ready for the next day which was Mother's Day. Obviously the people in attendance were rather limited since we did not advertise the occasion. Only Billie's close kin were there from Throckmorton and numbered about twenty. Rev. Tower, father of congressman John Tower, performed the ceremony. The service started about 11:00 pm and we were out of the church by midnight ready to go to our one night honeymoon at the Kemp Hotel.

R. & MRS. JOSEPH JURLINA LATE MAY 1945 IN THROCKMORT(

I had to report for duty again at 6:00 am on Monday following our wedding on Saturday to start another two-week field-problem similar to the one just before we married. Billie spent most of the next two weeks in Throckmorton subbing for a teacher who had quit her job. She then returned to Lawton to try find a place to live in a city that was filled with GI's wives trying to do the same thing. She stayed with a friend of a friend from Throckmorton. Needless to say it was tough and she finally managed to rent a one room, share-the-bath apartment in Lawton that was owned by a woman with a seven year old daughter and no husband. The bath was supposed to be shared but the woman "entertained" so many men that the bathroom door stayed locked from her side more than it was open for us to use.

That arrangement lasted for about three months until I made Staff Sergeant and we were able to get an apartment on the base for non-commissioned officers (NCOS). It was so LUXURIOUS compared to what we had just moved out of that we could not believe our luck. We had two bedrooms with army cots for beds, a living room, a kitchen and a nice bathroom. We bought about $50 worth of used furniture from a family that was being transferred. We were as happy as could be until we had to leave in January of 1946 to be separated from the service and go to Austin, Texas to enter the University of Texas.

ENGINEERING SCHOOL AT THE UNIVERSITY OF TEXAS

My discharge from the Army of the United States was finalized on 1 February 1946, at the Separation Center located at Camp Atterbury, Indiana (East of Terra Haute). The same day I hitched a ride, or better said, rides to my parent's home in Cleveland, Ohio, for a short visit. Meanwhile, my wife Billie had gone on to Austin, Texas, to look for an apartment or some place to live. Her cousin Kathryn Brown was then working as secretary to the then Lt. Governor John Lee Smith. It seemed that Billie was always the one to precede me to a new location. She was always the very best in locating places to live or making such arrangements.

Before going on with this bit of history we probably should discuss why we had decided to go to Austin and the University of Texas. For some weeks before my discharge we had checked with the Registrar at Ohio State University in Columbus, Ohio, to determine the situation there with respect to my entry as a student. The response was that there had been such a press of veterans trying to enroll, over 6,000 freshmen were scheduled for the first semester of the year, that housing was very critical thus the school could not accept any new students who did not have confirmed living quarters in which to start the semester.

As it turned out, the situation in Austin was much the same but my resourceful wife managed to find a one-bedroom garage-apartment behind the home of the owner of Hirsch Pharmacies in Austin. The home was at 1202 Castle Hill Street which is on the west side of Congress Avenue. As the street name indicates we were on top of a rather good hill which is fairly typical of Austin. With our financial situation being rather slender we walked everywhere we went in town and to and from the campus where Billie worked as a secretary in the Electrical Engineering

Joseph Jurlina

Research Laboratory (EERL) for various people involved with Radar Wave Propagation Studies for the U.S. Navy.

Calling what we had an apartment is a slight misnomer but it was home for a while and long enough to get situated. The servants' quarters consisted of one room with an alcove, called a bathroom, separated from the bed room by a curtain. The bedroom had a three-quarter bed, a small drop-leaf table, and two chairs we had at Fort Sill as well as a hotplate located in the bath room on which we cooked. All of our clothes had to be stored under our bed in our suitcases because there were no closets. A cardboard "closet" was later purchased for our hanging clothes. Billie often commented privately that the arrangement was very unique in that one could "sit on the pot and stir the beans" without getting up.

Our landlord and his wife were very nice to us and shortly after we moved in they went on an out-of-town trip which lasted for several days during which time they granted us full use of the their kitchen. One evening Billie was preparing our meal and had the surface units of the gas range in use and also turned the oven thermostat up anticipating the baking of biscuits. The oven had a pilot and automatic light-up feature. Unfortunately, and unknown to us the pilot was not operating too well, and this time failed by going out. Needless to say when Billie opened the oven door a few moments later the accumulation of gas was ignited by the surface units and the oven exploded in Billie's face.

Fortunately, although she was burned about the face with second degree burns and she lost a lot of hair she did not receive any scarring burns. I called an ambulance and she was rushed to the emergency room of Brackenridge Hospital where she was treated by a young physician by the name of S.H. (BUD) Dryden from west Texas. She stayed in the hospital for several days and to this day I cannot remember how we managed to pay the bills.

After Billie's burns healed we continued to use Dr. Dryden as our family doctor throughout our stay in Austin. In fact, when Billie discovered she was pregnant a few weeks after her hospital stay she used Dr. Dryden as her doctor and it was he who delivered Carol Ann, our first child, in Brackenridge Hospital. Back in those dark days of the past, doctors made house-calls and on more than one occasion when Dr. Dryden came to our home he would linger in conversation because, we decided much later, he was trying to get relief from the hectic pace of the day with patients.

Years later Dr. S.H. (Bud) Dryden was elected to the Council of the City of Austin, Texas. Exactly when he served I am not certain, but it must have been in the late sixties or early seventies. Dr. Dryden practiced medicine in Austin at least until early 1990. My research shows that he died in the mid-nineties.

Getting back to the principal theme of this chapter, I enrolled in the Engineering School hoping to become an Electrical Engineer, All my life I had been impressed by the professionalism of the engineers I had met and because my interests had always been in things electrical. I am sure that had I met a successful accountant early in my childhood my inclination might have been to go another way. Following that line of thought, I now wish that I had met a bright insurance or real estate person because in the times in which Billie and I have grown up the opportunities in those fields seemed to have been phenomenal.

As I recall, in my first semester at UT the registrar would not grant me full credit for the 42 hours we had received in the ASTP work at NTSTC in Denton so I found myself taking second semester Freshman English along with Texas History and Government which was required. My course load amounted to about seventeen hours and I did manage to pass everything in spite of having been out of school for two years. My grades were not spectacular but passing was important. By the time summer rolled around and I enrolled for the summer sessions Billie was obviously pregnant, and we had to start thinking about supplementing our income, with my going into productive employment, because we knew Billie would stay home with our child for some time in the future. As it turned out I did some part-time work in the same lab Billie worked in until November when Carol Ann was born. For the rest of my time at UT I worked about half-time, arranging my classes in the mornings and leaving my afternoons free to work at the EERL. In the last semester, and it may have two semesters, Billie went back to work at the lab while I kept Carol Ann in the afternoons. Carol Ann was in a nursery for the mornings only.

My responsibilities in the lab were to act as an aide (gofer) for the engineers in processing data collected in their research projects. Oftentimes, they needed photographs of the equipment used and it turned out I was the only one who needed the job bad enough to do the work. During this time, part-time students were raking in the fantastic sum of sixty-five cents an hour. Much later the rate went up to ninety cents. We managed to survive with this income coupled with the GI Bill student allotment of $120 dollars a month for married veterans with children. Of course, Mom and Pop Grable (Willie Laura and John Francis) managed to assist us considerably with their frequent deliveries of frozen beef from their locker and sacks of dried red beans. Without their assistance I am sure we would have had to resort to bologna (our round steak) much more often than we did.

We must mention another great contribution to our survival during our school days in Austin, Texas and that was the blessing of meeting Mr. & Mrs. Carroll and Mollie Smith. Mom & Pop as we were wont to refer to them were the parents of Carroll Smith, Jr. who, as a B-17 Pilot, was killed early in WWII. We met Mom & Pop through Sylvia Smith, widow of Carroll, Jr. who attended the First Methodist Church in Austin as did Billie. Mom & Pop were very generous people who had us as guests in their home for Sunday lunch and hundreds of other times during our stay in Austin. They were obviously the most sincere Christian couple we had ever met. Shortly before Carol Ann was born on 25 November 1946, we were lucky enough to get an apartment for married veterans that the University had built with some federal assistance money. Brackenridge Apartments were located on West 6th Street just across the street (West) from the Austin Municipal Golf Course. Our address was 1206-A from October 1946 until we left Austin in February 1950 following my graduation. The structures were made of WWII officers-quarters salvaged from various military installations in Texas. When the Apartments were constructed they were called temporary quarters but they were in continuous use until the eighties when they were removed from the property and replaced with more permanent housing.

CITY BOY

All things considered my experience at the University of Texas in the Engineering School was great but not what it might have been had it not been for the large number of new students, mostly veterans of WWII, in most of my classes. It was obvious that all Departments were not prepared for the size of the student body and as a result the teaching staff was not what one would expect in a first class university. Way too many classes were taught by graduate students with very little experience or training in the teaching process. Many knew the material fairly well but could not communicate their material well enough to suit me and many of my peers.

OUR HOME IN AUSTIN, TX FROM OCT. 1946 TIL JANUARY 1950 AT 1206A

You might recall that earlier in this epistle I mentioned driving a truck while in the service. To that point I had not driven any kind of vehicle; however, sometime in 1949 Billie's father, John Francis Grable, agreed to sell us his 1939 two-door Chevrolet coupe because he was planning to buy a new 1950 model Mercury. I believe he asked $300 for it and right now I cannot recall how we ever paid him for the vehicle. Billie taught me all I know about driving and I finally took the driving exam in Austin, Travis County, Texas to get my license.

I did have to take a written test which I passed quite easily and made a perfect score. Then I took an actual driving test with a Texas Highway Patrolman sitting in the passenger seat. This was exciting for a couple of reasons. First, I had not done too much driving so I was not very confident I could do what was required of me. Second, the 1939 model car was not in perfect condition and I was not certain that it might not just stop on me in the process of the test. As it turned out I was doing absolutely fine until the officer asked me to start back to the testing office. As soon as I made my first right turn the horn on the car starting to

blow and didn't stop until I straightened out around the corner so the officer said "that will be 5% off your grade" and then asked me to head back to the testing office. In the process of returning I had to make three more turns and believe it or not the horn blew during each turn, something it had never done before this test. The officer's only comment was "it's a good thing you did not have to make another turn or two

CITY BOY

because I had to deduct 5% for each time the horn blew which would have caused you to fail the test". As it turned out I received my first driver's license at age twenty five in the fall of 1949. To this day, Billie brags about how she had taught me all I know about driving.

OUR FIRSTBORN - CAROL ANN JURLINA

As I mentioned in the last chapter, Billie discovered she was "that way" early in my first semester at the University. It was very strange how I could feel shock, unbelief, joy and anticipation all at the same time but I did and I knew things were going to be different from that time on. Billie kept working at the EERL through her pregnancy until about two weeks before Carol Ann was born not because she or I wanted her to, but because her earnings were a very significant part of our income and livelihood.

About the time Billie resigned her position, I had started working part-time at the EERL and after her leaving it looked like my working hours would have to be increased. At the start of the fall semester I made the mistake of registering for eighteen hours of course-work thinking that we could manage all that had to be done. Of course, I discovered very soon how I had erred because there just were not enough hours for the studying I should have done so I dropped one course. Unfortunately, I waited too late to discover I should have dropped two courses and ended up with an "F" in an engineering course I had to have credit in to graduate. I repeated that course later on and passed without too much difficulty.

The 25th of November 1946 in Austin started out like almost every other school day. I went to my classes that morning and had my peanut-butter & jelly "sandwich", or something that exotic for lunch, and caught the bus out to the EERL lab to work in the afternoon. About two hours into the afternoon I received a call from one of our neighbors saying that Billie was being taken to Brackenridge Hospital by Mary and Johnny Peacock because Billie had started her labor. Well, there I was afoot in Manor, Texas, where the lab was located and about ten miles from the hospital. Nothing to do, I waited for the next bus to the campus, and then transferred to the bus going to the hospital. A process that must have taken at least two hours but I can not swear to these facts since I was quite nervous.

Dr. Sam H. (Bud) Dryden was there when I arrived and let me know the status of things but I could not see Billie since she was in a labor room. Billie later described it as a labor arena where there were 10-12 girls all going through the same process and not all enjoying what was happening. Anyway, this labor process went on until

CAROL ANN WITH DAD JOE ABT APRIL 1947

Carol Ann was delivered at 11:46 P.M. on 25 November 1946, or as the avid Texas University fans used to say "Turkey Day Eve". To say that I was not prepared to be a parent is an understatement. I was excited and relieved that things turned out OK and happy, but definitely not prepared.

A day or so after Billie came home from the hospital, which in those days was about five days after the child was delivered, Billie's

GRANDMOTHER MARY TELBAN JURLINA WITH CAROL ANN SUMMER 1947 IN AUSTIN, TX

sister Louise Boyd, came to Austin to help us through the first few days of parenting until Billie was back on her feet. One day while Billie was breast-feeding Carol Ann down stairs, both of them went to sleep, and Billie awoke to find Carol Ann choking on milk and turning blue. I was in the bathroom upstairs when I heard Louise and Billie scream for help. I came bounding down the one flight of stairs in one or two steps at most in time to have Carol Ann thrust into my arms. Carol Ann was pretty blue looking so I turned her face down in my left hand with her head pointed downward and patted her with my right hand until she started complaining with a slight wimper or two. To this day I'm not sure whether she was actually choking or simply asleep but I do know that I died three or four times before it looked like she started breathing normally again. From that time on, until she was two or three, feeding her was always an ordeal for me.

The early years of Carol Ann's life was spent in and around Brackenridge Apartments with many other children of the same age born to veterans all back in school trying to catch up on their educations. One of her closest friends was Sandra Kay Veigel, oldest daughter of Ren and Edward Veigel, a law student. Carol Ann and Sandy played together daily to the point that many people mistook them for twins or sisters or

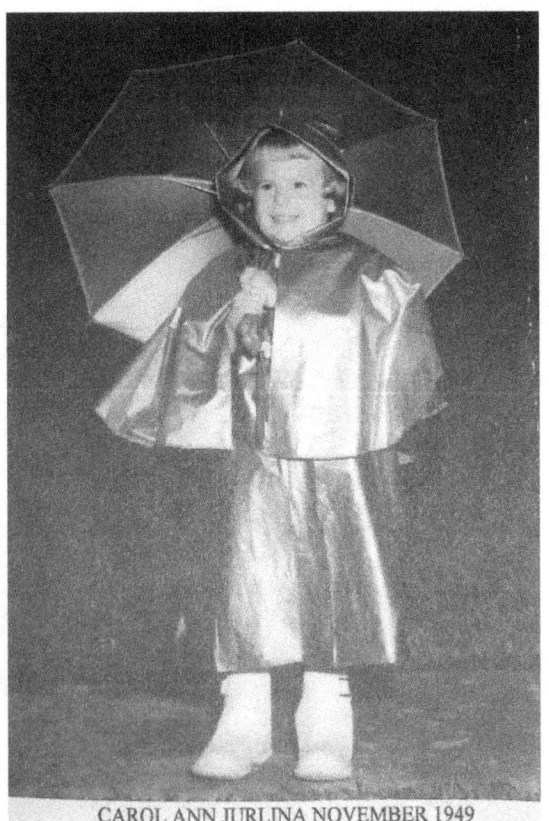

CAROL ANN JURLINA NOVEMBER 1949

both. Ed & Ren had four children: Sandra, Patty, David, and Paul. Ed Veigel graduated with his Law Degree and for more than fifty years was a partner in the law firm of Boyd, Veigel and Gay. Ed was a navigator in a B-17 during the WWII and was shot down while over Germany. He was wounded and returned to the States for treatment and rehabilitation. He was a victim of pancreatic cancer and died in 2004 in McKinney, Texas.

Johnny & Mary Peacock were next door neighbors of ours and had a son, Johnny Byron Peacock, their first born in Austin. The son played pro-football for the New England Patriots. The second son, Ronny, I believe also played pro-football. A third son, Randy, was born after the Peacocks left Austin. Mr. Peacock Senior was School Superintendant at Goliad, Texas for years and retired in 1985.

James Russell & Netty.were also neighbors and they had Gaylene and Russell. James Russell horn has practiced law in Austin, Texas for several years. Gaylene lives in Austin, Texas.

Lemuel L & Beth LaRue were across the street neighbors in Austin at the Brackenridge Apartments with their daughter Kay Beth. Sister Connie was born in Austin before Mr. LaRue completed his college work and they moved to Denton, Texas. Kay Beth is now a school pincipal in Garland, Texas and she is married to Eckhart Kuner who was born in Germany. LaRue, as we called him, completed his course work before we did and he and his family moved to Denton, Texas where Beth, Mrs. L.L. Larue grew up. LaRue served on the staff at the Women's College and ended up as chief financial officer there. During WWII LaRue was a forward observer for the artillery of the 102nd Infantry Division.. A description of his background as a pilot and his service is included in the Appendix to this report.

CITY BOY

I should mention here that just before my discharge from the Army of the U. S. A. I signed up for a three-year term in the Army Reserve just in case I needed to "re-up" in the service. Fortunately, my term in the reserves ended in 1949 while I was still a student at the University in Austin, Texas. The Korean War did not break out until about the middle of June 1950.

GRADUATION AND MY FIRST POSITION

Graduation from the University and the earning of a B.S.E.E. was rather an important event taking place on 30 January 1950, but without our presence because we were involved in trying to find gainful employment. The arrangement on our Brackenridge Apartment was that we had to be full-time students and as of the end of that fall semester I was no longer a student. I had always dreamed about having a big blowout upon graduation but at the time it seemed more important to find a job and a place to live for the family. Not only that but we could not afford a blowout of any magnitude anyway.

In spite of all the interviews on campus, only six members of our Electrical Engineering Class had confirmed employment before leaving the campus, and if my memory serves me right the six were in the very top of our class. Needless to say, I was not in the top of the class but far enough up to be in the running in normal times. Engineers were a dime a dozen in February but by June when the Korean War was heating up the search for Engineers of all kinds became very frantic. So frantic, that after accepting employment and even changing jobs I received telephone calls with some rather interesting offers but too late to make another family move across country. A couple of classmates who come to mind in discussing those who had accepted job offers prior to graduation include Perry G. Brittain and Jack T. Nipper. As I recall Perry accepted an offer from Dallas Power & Light and Jack accepted the offer from IBM. Perry went on to become Chairman of the Board of Texas Utilities Company and retired about the same time I did. Jack was with IBM for several years but I have lost track of him. Perry died about 2005.

I forgot to mention the job offer I had from the Lower Colorado River Authority (LCRA) just before graduation which I accepted and then had to withdraw my acceptance. LCRA was in the process of building the dam on the Colorado River at Marble Falls, Texas, and needed an Electrical Inspector to bird-dog the contractors. The job seemed like a good way to get into the organization so I accepted. Billie and I drove to Marble Falls to look for a place to live and found an apartment that we thought would do for a while. When we got back to Austin Billie came down with asthmatic-bronchitis which the doctor felt was aggravated by her allergy to Cedar pollen which in the hill country is very bad during the late fall and early winter. Our doctor told Joe if he wanted Billie to live, we would have to move. No allergy medications were available at that time. So, we had to let LCRA know we could not stay in that part of Texas.

We interviewed several other companies but to no avail until sometime in early April, when West Texas Utilities finally offered me a job in their meter testing group in Abilene, Texas. The man who hired me was a "former student" of A&M by the name of J. F..Longley. Mr. Longley promised me the next opening in the Engineering Department. We worked in the meter group for a couple of months when I was asked to move to McCamey, Texas, as a Substation Operator, in what was a switching point in the WTU system. Again, I was promised the next opening in the Engineering Department so I accepted the transfer to the wilds of far West Texas.

The job was not much of a challenge but it did give me another opportunity to see how a transmission system functioned first hand. The people in McCamey were super and we really enjoyed the peace and quiet of living in a Company Camp for employees on the East side of town and in effect our own little community of about ten families. McCamey at that time had the dubious honor of having the highest municipal water rates of any community in Texas and, therefore, very few homes in town had any grass or shrubbery around them. However, at the Camp the water was supplied by company-owned deep wells so we had all the water we could use. In addition, the electrical energy for our home was not metered and free. While the salary was minimal the other factors made the place reasonably comfortable and certainly different than anything I had experienced aside from camping out in the Army.

CITY BOY

The night before we were to move, Billie had a miscarriage. I had to leave her in the hospital to meet Mom Grable and Louise in Abilene to hand off Carol Ann. Consequently, I preceded Billie and Carol Ann to McCamey by a week or two. The house we had was a shotgun affair with a hallway which ran from front to back with rooms on either side. The first night I decided to sleep in the hallway so that the cool breeze might make the sleeping tolerable because it was very warm. Imagine my surprise, when long before midnight I was awakened by the sensation of freezing to death only to find that in the desert climate and at an elevation of about 2500 ft. the temperature had dropped 30-35 degrees.

VISIT TO McCAMEY, TEXAS
IN APRIL 1988
WHERE JOE WAS EMPLOYED
BY W.T.U. IN 1950

WE LIVED IN HOUSE COMPARABLE FROM APRIL THRU AUGUST 1950
SUBSATATION IS WHERE JOE ACTED AS OPERATOR AND DISPATCHER
1950 POPULATION OF MCCAMEY WAS ABOUT HALF OF THAT IN 1988

It was while we were in McCamey that we had the chance to spend several weekends in the Davis Mountains and Balmorhea, Reeves County area where the Indian Springs are located. Late spring or fall in these places, when they have had some good rains, is a great experience and one especially suited for photography. Very shortly after we moved into our new home I acquired a Border Colley puppy for Carol Ann that turned out to be a great little pet. As I recall, it was given to me in San Angelo on my way to McCamey from Abilene but exactly how it came about slips my mind now. Later on, when we moved from McCamey to Cleveland, we had to leave the dog behind because of the uncertainty of the housing in

Cleveland. This distressed Carol Ann more than the rest of us but it was a very traumatic experience for all.

We had not been in McCamey too many months when a "Primary Meterman" from Abilene came through one day showing off a brand new Aggie employee from the Engineering Department. When I discovered that he had just been added to the payroll in a job which I had been promised and I had not been given the opportunity to decline the opening, to say that I was disturbed and upset is an understatement. So, before that day was too much older I called Mr. Longley and let him know how little I thought about his ability to keep a promise and how disappointed I was. Later that evening, my brother Tom called from Cleveland, Ohio, to see how we were doing in far West Texas and to report his situation with a new consulting business for which he was working as a part-time employee. They were subcontracting the engineering and design of machines used to manufacture the Walker Bulldog Tank for U.S. Army. Anyway, I unloaded my frustration about my job on Tom.

The very next day, to my surprise, I received a telephone call from a Lee W. McClellan, owner of Process Machine & Tool Company, the company that Tom had been working with for some time. Before our conversation had gone much more than five minutes Lee McClellan offered me a job. Not only was the job going to be more of a challenge than the one we had but the opportunity to work a considerable amount of overtime meant more income immediately. The next day, after talking it over with my wife, we called him back and promised to be in Cleveland as soon as I could after giving Mr. Longley two weeks notice.

It was obvious that my former employer realized he had screwed up royally by giving the Aggie my job but his protestations and promises fell on deaf ears. That was one of the few times in my life that I felt good about telling another person that they had made a serious mistake and that I did not and would not accept such treatment from a person who considered himself a professional. To make a long story short I made it to Cleveland, Ohio, about the first of September while Billie and Carol Ann stopped in Throckmorton, Texas, to stay with Billie's parents until November.

CITY BOY

MY SECOND POSITION

As mentioned previously, I preceded Billie and Carol Ann to Cleveland to Process Machine & Tool Company and to give Billie a chance to visit with her parents. Our furniture was shipped ahead and placed in storage until we could find a place to live. Before we review that though, I should describe my reaction as I drove my 1948 4-door Chevrolet Sedan from McCamey to Cleveland, Ohio, in the fall of 1950. You will recall that I left Cleveland on 17 March 1943 and except for brief visits had not been home many times or for any length of time until this trip in 1950; so for more than seven years I had been separated from the environment of Cleveland.

As I was driving back home, the thing which stood out most in my observations as I crossed the Mississippi River and got closer to home was that the cities and towns seemed to look older, dirtier and more run down than those I had gotten used to seeing in Texas and the Southwest. When I came to the outskirts of Cleveland I really felt like a stranger going into a land totally unfamiliar and foreign. By the time I drove north on Norwood from Superior Avenue and then made the turn onto Carl Avenue and finally onto East 63rd Street where my parents lived, I knew I had made a great big mistake. The streets seemed so narrow and the entire neighborhood looked so soot-covered and grimy that I felt uneasy just thinking about having to establish a home there and bring my family into such an unfamiliar and strange environment. If our furniture had not already been shipped and in storage, I believe I might have turned around and gone back to Texas without too much discussion. Well, I did not turn around and before too many months after Billie and Carol Ann came down we settled in and enjoyed our living there.

Process Machine & Tool Company was what is called in the trade a *job-shop consulting company* concentrating on those manufacturing firms whose design and engineering forces were tied up either taking care of their own product lines or were tied up in government orders and did not have enough manpower to take care of additional jobs with short-term deadlines. Or said another way, rather than adding manpower for jobs which might not last but a few weeks or months the manufacturer would use us for these projects as an extension of their staffs, they paid a premium for the service cost-wise but were willing to absorb the cost to maintain their reputations for good service in the industry.

Upstairs was home for a while

Snow Rd - Parma, Ohio

When I joined Process Machine & Tool Company there were only about 12-14 employees including the owner and a Secretary. My brother Tom was working part time and going to school at what was then Case Institute of Technology, now part of Case-Western Reserve University. The big project in the house and the main reason for my being hired was a contract with Wean Equipment Company to design several machines to be used in the manufacture of Walker Bulldog T41-E1 Tanks equipped with a 76mm high velocity gun. Wean was a primary subcontractor for the Cadillac Motor Car Division of General Motors Corporation who had the contract to build the tanks in the Cleveland Tank Plant, a building used during WWII for aircraft manufacture.

Our projects consisted of a grinding machine, a drilling machine and a milling machine all to be used to prepare and finish the bogey suspension pads on the side of the tank where the drive tracks are mounted. The hull, or "part" as we called it, at the stage of manufacture we received it consisted of a rough hull with the turret-ring, mounted and machined to establish a centerline about the turret center for further machining. Our machines were to grind the suspension pads to certain dimensions with reference to the turret-ring, drill holes in the pads for mounting the suspension systems and mill special-shaped openings in the pads. My specific assignment in all this was to design the hydraulic system to be used on the grinding machine. This system was then adapted to the two other machines because of the similarity of function on the same portion of the "part".

The grinding machine was to consist of two similar sections, one on either side of the tank hull. Each section had five grinding heads mounted on a cast-iron slide which could be retracted from the side of the hull to facilitate loading and unloading the hull in an upside-down position on a locating plug in the center of the turret ring. Overall size of the machine was about 55 feet in width, 70 feet in length, 18 feet in height and a total weight of over 350 tons. Total motor capacity in grinding heads and hydraulic pumps was about 600 hp in ten motors. Each of the ten coolant pumps for the grinding operation could deliver 700 gallons of special coolant per minute. Before the completion of our machines the production of finished tank hulls was limited to one per eight-hour shift, but after our machines were placed in operation the production increased to one hull every 42 minutes.

Two incidents which occurred during the design and erection of the machines come to mind. The first happened shortly after my hydraulic control panel design was completed. On all the drawings of machine components we always placed a large red-stamped message which clearly stated that, because of its size, the machine had to be assembled in its final resting place and not constructed in one place and moved to its final destination (N.B.: ASSEMBLE ON SITE). On the day in mind I received a telephone call from one of the Wean people telling me how they had trouble picking up the control panels in their shop. It seemed that they assembled the panels in their shop and in trying to lift the panels to load them on large flatbed trucks, they put lifting-slings under each end of the panel which was 25 feet long, about 5 feet deep, 8 feet high and weighed about 5-6 tons. As the crane lifted the panels the middle of the panel stayed on the plant floor and they could not understand why that should happen. Of course, I reminded them about the note "to build in place" but it was too late to admonish them on that point so I suggested that a platform of eight-inch I-beams, as a minimum, be made and welded to the bottom of the panels for lifting and transportation to the Tank Plant.

The second incident happened about one week after the final assembly of the grinding machine had taken place and production testing had started. I received a call asking that my brother Tom and I come out to the Tank Plant to see how well things were proceeding, so we made our way to the production line to visit with the machine operator on duty. Without telling him that we had designed the machine, we simply told him we were asked to look the machine over and look for possible minor improvements which might be made to facilitate production and use. He immediately stated that the machine was working great and running very smoothly but he had to make some adjustment of the coolant hoses to direct the flow of liquid where it did the most good. He commented that he could not understand how the *"engineers who designed the machine could have missed the placement of hoses"*. We asked if he had enough hose and room for adjustment to which he responded that he had plenty. As Tom and I were leaving we each commented that obviously the bold red message on the blueprints were again ignored for each print had the same message *"Adjust Hoses To Suit After Grinding Heads are In Place"* printed in red.

All in all, the experience on this tank project was one of the most enlightening experiences we had during our time at Process Machine. We learned that all problems can be solved in more than one way and any machine or tool must be designed so that in fact the machine or tool can be made as designed. If the erection or manufacture of the product is so complex that not every mortal can understand the process then appropriate instructions must be developed. In many cases this is done by the designer as he progresses just to make certain a redo is not necessary. Another thing which was also apparent after a little time on the project was the fact that not many engineers of any field were involved in design work in most companies like ours. Lee W. McClellan was unique in that way too. Having one or two highly trained individuals on his staff just in case was important.

By the time I finished the control panel design, our shop had about 80-plus people on the payroll and we were really cranking out the work in a hurry. So much so that we were running out of jobs to keep our employee-staff fully occupied, so Lee McClellan put three of his people on the road trying to drum up additional design business. I was the third member of this team and a rather reluctant one to boot but it had to be done and I could see the benefits to seeing other operations in the selling process.

In our design room we had been working six days a week, 8:00 am till 10:00 pm Monday through Friday and 8:00 am till 6:00 pm on Saturday. The hours were tough but the pay was exceptionally good and at a time we needed everything we could get. The hours on the road were much the same except that the evening hours were used for traveling or preparing schedules and information for the next day. In the year or so on the road I averaged about 60,000 miles a year between Chicago and New York City and made anywhere from five to eight calls in a day.

Of course, selling a service such as ours to me was more difficult than selling a product of any kind. We had nothing concrete to show except our willingness to perform and the written comments of appreciation our past customers had been considerate enough to write. I met a large number of extremely capable people in my visits in the offices of plant managers and chief engineers in that very manufacturing-oriented part of the United States. In the 12-14 months that I traveled, I found many places I would really have wanted to spend more time in, and in fact many where I would have loved to have worked. For what seemed like a long time my efforts selling did not seem to bear any fruit but I noticed that the other salesmen were not doing any better.

Finally, one day Lee McClellan called me into his office and suggested that I should spend more money than I had been because my expenses were significantly less than the other sales people. I told him I was doing with our busy potential clients, what I would hope they might do for us and that was not waste too much of their time trying to wine and dine them. He was not much satisfied with my explanation but did not press the issue at that time. Within a month of our conversation several of my clients called and asked for special revisits from me or with Lee to discuss projects on which they wanted help. Meanwhile the other two salesmen had not generated any business and within the next thirty days both were removed from our payroll because some investigation had revealed that they had not been working very diligently.

One of the customers that wanted help from us, was the Harrison Radiator Division of General Motors located in Lockport, New York. They were involved in the manufacture of parts for the exhaust-end of fighter-jet engines and needed help to keep schedules on welding fixture design. We started our association with Harrison Radiator in 1952 and on a visit to Cleveland in the late nineteen seventies discovered they were still a happy customer.

The overall job situation at Process Machine & Tool Company was pretty good and a great place to get a lot of experience in a hurry. However, while we were in Cleveland Billie's father died in March of 1952 and her brother John was diagnosed with cancer of the lower intestine in that same year. In addition, Billie was pregnant with Michael and she was obviously quite anxious about a child about to be born outside of Texas so we decided that with all things considered we ought to move back to Texas before our second child was born. This decision was made in July 1952 and I planned to return to Dallas, TX to look for a job in mid August while Billie and Carol Ann visited with her family in Throckmorton, Throckmorton County, Texas, for a few weeks.

During our visit to Cleveland in November 1991, Process Machine & Tool Company was still listed in the telephone directory although the principle owner, Lee W. McClellan, died a few years before, about 1989. I assume that the employees had bought out Mr. McClellan or he had sold out sometime after my Brother Tom's death in 1967.

CITY BOY

MY THIRD POSITION

As mentioned in the previous chapter after the decision to come back to Texas was made in July of 1952 Billie and Carol Ann preceded me by two or three weeks and stayed with Mrs. J. F. Grable, Billie's mother, in Throckmorton. I stayed on the job until my obligations in projects were satisfied and drove back to Texas sometime in early August in our 1950 Plymouth sedan which had about 60,000 miles on it.

We decided early on that we were going to locate in Dallas this time around so I made a couple of trips to Dallas from Throckmorton interviewing various companies without too much encouragement. I believe it was on my second trip to Dallas that I went to Dallas Power & Light Company to see what if anything was going on there but got a real cold shoulder. Having been rejected at DP&L I decided to go to lunch in the bus station just south of the DP&L building and as I passed the building directory I spotted the name Texas Power & Light Company so I noted the room number posted for the Personnel Department and went on to lunch.

Later, when I reached the TP&L offices I was informed that the Personnel Manager, Tom Sewell, was out of the city but I could visit with a William E. Reeder. Bill Reeder was a very personable young man about 4-5 years my junior who asked me the questions one would expect and then had me fill out an employment application form. Having done that, they took me to the Engineering Department offices to visit with the Chief Engineer, T.D. Thomas. Much later I discovered his initials stood for Talmage DeWitt. He was a graduate of Rice Institute and obviously a true gentleman.

Mr. Thomas visited with me for thirty minutes or so and then asked what sort of starting salary I had in mind. I told him what I had made in my previous employment in Cleveland and told him that I would have to have at least $325 per month. He seemed a bit surprised and countered that such an amount was higher than he was paying some of his Engineers already on the payroll. I suggested as nicely as I could that perhaps he was not paying them enough because, with the cost of living being what it was, I could not work for less. He asked me to visit with a Mr. W. D.

Joseph Jurlina

Kelsey who at that time was in charge of the Transmission Design Section. After Mr. Kelsey was through talking to me I was told to return to Mr. Thomas's office. My visit with Bill Kelsey was not very productive and I decided if offered a position in that group I would decline and go elsewhere.

Fortunately, I was asked to visit with another engineer about three years my junior by the name of Ted L. Hatcher who was supervising a group of engineers in the System Planning Division. It seems that Ted had been at Texas A&M conducting some system studies on an analog system analyzer and had just come back into Dallas for some new data and was about to drive back to College Station when Mr. Thomas intercepted him in the hallway and asked him to speak to this young man looking for a job.

Ted talked to me and while doing so noticed the $325 I had asked for in salary but as I remember he said nothing to me about it until years later. I was taken back to Mr. Thomas after Ted and I had our *conflab* and Mr. Thomas again asked me about the $325 and would I take any less. Again I reminded him that the rate we were discussing represented a cut of 50% from my average monthly earnings in the last twelve months. In the next five minutes I was hired and filled out all the forms necessary for me to be placed on the payroll effective 1 September 1952, at a monthly rate of $325 per month, as a conditional employee to work in the System Engineering Division with Ted Hatcher as my supervisor and Mr. John B. Robuck as the Division Manager.

Some years later, I discovered that TP&L had some trouble hiring new people because the starting salaries and even salaries for those on the payroll for some years lagged the salaries being paid in the industry. I was hired at a rate which was $75 higher than Ted's and he had been on the payroll over two years before I arrived on the scene. As soon as Ted came back to town from A&M the next week he stormed into Mr. Robuck's office and offered to resign immediately unless his salary were adjusted to a proper level. We joked afterward that I was responsible for his first very significant raise.

Initially, my job in the System Engineering Division was to become familiar with the TP&L system and be able to recognize the names and locations of

CITY BOY

all power plants and major switching stations without having to look at a map. Additionally, I was to become familiar in how the basic data were prepared for the system modeling which was done for use on the A&M network analyzer. The data and concepts were quite a bit different than that which I had been doing at Process Machine but with Ted's help and some digging we were able to refresh our mind and get up to speed in what I hoped was a reasonable time. Years later I was able to draw from memory the entire transmission system and spot all the plants and switching stations on our system and those of all the interconnected systems and almost all the load serving distribution substations on our system. In fact, in time I could recall the size of conductor on all the transmission lines in our system and if pressed could draw the switching arrangement in all TP&L major switching stations. In some quarters, especially among the new employees, I was referred to as the walking TP&L transmission encyclopedia.

About seven weeks after joining the TP&L staff our second child Michael Kenneth Jurlina was born on 20 October 1952. At that time we were living on Dearborn Street in the Oak Cliff part of Dallas about eight miles southwest of downtown Dallas on the west side of the Trinity River. We had contracted to buy a tract house under construction at 2727 Wilbur Street but it was not to be completed until sometime in November.

As I recall we moved into our 1070 square foot $10,500 California-style home with a slab foundation and oak flooring just before Christmas 1952. Our lot was a pie-shaped affair about 70 feet across the front and over 200 feet deep on one side and just under 200 feet on the other side, and about 150 feet across the back. Our lot backed up to a railroad which turned out to be a good neighbor for the children.

The oak flooring in the entire house was nailed to 1" x 2" wide wood sleepers which in turn were "stuck" to the slab with an asphalt compound. I was somewhat leery of the floors to begin with and sure enough after the drought of the fifties ended in 1957, moisture worked its way up through the slab because they had not placed a vapor barrier between the ground and the slab. Within a short while the oak floors began to warp and there was not much one could do but put up with the situation or tear out the flooring and improvise. Fortunately we only put up with the wavy floor until 1962 but that's another story.

OUR SECONDBORN - MICHAEL KENNETH JURLINA

Michael Kenneth Jurlina was born shortly before Noon on 20 October 1952 in the Florence Nightingale wing of Baylor Hospital located at 3500 Gaston Avenue in Dallas, Dallas County, Texas. Michael was delivered by Asa A. Newsom, MD, in what was then the maternity wing of Baylor. It was demolished shortly after Michael's birth to make room for the great expansion of the hospital - an expansion which seems to continue unabated today.

The day on which Michael decided to make his appearance started out like any other Monday but livened up very soon after we arose that morning. About 6:30 am I had started to shave when Billie said something to the effect that I had better hurry because she was having some pains that were indicative that *"the time"* had come. So, we took Carol Ann, who was almost six at the time, next door to our neighbors and started our drive toward Baylor Hospital which from our rent home on Walker Street in Cockrell Hill was about 8-9 miles away.

Traffic during the morning rush hour in Dallas at that time, and ever since for that matter, was heavy and frantic it seemed to me. When we started across the Trinity River on the Jefferson Street Viaduct the inbound traffic was set at three lanes and the outbound traffic cut down to one lane. The inbound lanes were full and moving rather slowly and every minute or so Billie would urge me to hurry along. Finally, in desperation, I looked down the outbound lane and saw it was clear so I turned on my headlights, sounded my horn, and took off in the fourth lane headed the wrong way toward town. I am sure I was not traveling very fast but at least three times faster than the traffic was then moving. We continued that way, lights on and horn blowing, all the way to Baylor in the hopes that a mounted policeman might be attracted and come along to find out the problem but to no avail. We made it to the hospital by about 7:30 am without encountering any police, and breaking at least ten driving rules.

CITY BOY

Dr. Newsom was in the hospital awaiting our arrival and in just a few minutes had Billie in a labor room where I was permitted to stay with my wife. We had not been there more than 30 minutes when Billie complained about her feet being cold and asked for a blanket. Dr. Newsom came in about the time we were putting another warm blanket over her feet so Billie commented about cold feet. At that point, Dr. Newsom looked at her and smiled as he said *"It's a hell of a time to get cold feet lady"!*

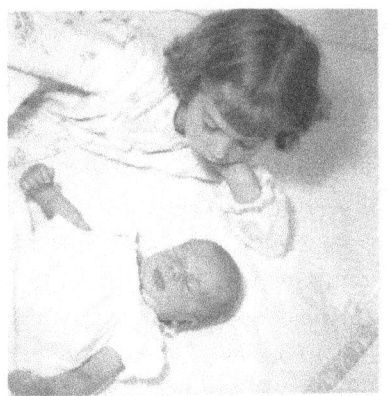

CAROL ANN WITH BROTHER MICHAEL   MICHAEL WITH DAD JOE AT 2727 WILBUR
OCTOBER 1952

After we were assured that mother and baby were OK I went home to pick up Carol Ann and took her to McKinney to stay with our long-time college-friends Edward and Ren Veigel. Billie's brother John Aaron Grable was critically ill with cancer of the lower intestine and, therefore, neither Billie's mother nor her sister could be with us. Billie and Michael came home the following Saturday at which time the Veigel's also brought Carol Ann back home to see her little brother for the first time. As I recall, she was excited about Michael but somewhat reserved and confused by this new member of the family who was getting so much attention from everyone around.

For about two weeks after Billie came home we had a neighbor lady stay with Billie and the children while I was at the office each day. John Aaron Grable died on 29 October 1952 and we were not able to attend his funeral because the doctor did not want Billie traveling the 180 miles in a car. Some time after the funeral, Grandmother Grable, a title she did not really enjoy having for some reason, came and stayed with us for a couple of weeks. The older grandchildren called her "Mama" so our children followed suit.

FIRST OWNED HOME LOCATED AT 2727 WILBUR ST. DALLAS 1952 – 1962

Michael was born in October before we moved into our new home in December. The new home was a California style one-story frame on a slab foundation located at 2727 Wilbur Street in Dallas, Dallas County, Texas. This slab foundation construction was new in Dallas at that time, and we were excited about the prospects of living in our first new home. We stayed there until July 1962, when Mike was almost ten and Carol Ann was almost sixteen. We moved to Sherman, Grayson County, Texas, for me to assume the District Manager's post for TP&L.

Michael grew up with a good many children but the ones which come to mind include: Randy Boone whose family moved to Duncanville, Texas, a few years before we moved to Sherman; Vicki Jett, Mary McFarland, David Red, Judy and Kathy Smith.

Randy Boone is now (2009) living in Hendersonville, North Carolina, and according to our last word on the staff at Kanuga, an Episcopal Center, after having been an ordained minister in the Presbyterian Church. Mary McFarland never married and in 1993 was living in her childhood home on Wilbur. Judy Ann Smith, born 1 February 1948, married (Chaney) and has two children, David and Jason. She died of cancer sometime ago. Kathy Sue Smith, born 28 September 1950, married (Lyon) and has two children, Misty and Christi, now lives in DeSoto, Texas. .We have no idea where

CITY BOY

MICHAEL & DAD IN SELF-PORTRAIT –

Vicki Jett is now living although we know that her mother Betty has died and Lance Jett, Vicki's father, has remarried.

A SECOND CHANCE TO GO BACK TO CLEVELAND

Some 6-7 years after we moved to Dallas, about 1959, I received a telephone call one day from Lee W. McClellan telling me he was in town on business and asking if Billie and I would like to have dinner with him. We arranged to meet him at a restaurant and had a great time reciting all the things that had happened along the way since the fall of 1952 when we left Cleveland. By this time I was in the office of Lee E. Cook, Vice President and Assistant General Manager of TP&L, acting as his administrative assistant without title.

A month or so after our visit with Lee W. McClellan in Dallas he called again and asked if I had any interest in coming back to Cleveland to assist him in his company. Although he did not specifically say, I believe he had some projects lined up in Texas that he felt would best be handled by someone familiar with the territory. I explained that my situation in Lee Cook's office looked pretty good and I hated to leave at that particular juncture without giving it a chance to develop. He respected my concern but suggested that a big company like TP&L was in a good position to abuse their hold on its employees as he had discovered first hand in

Detroit some years before. It was not until 1983-4 when what he had said started to come back to mind when TP&L, in the Texas Utilities Company reorganization, began to lose its influence and stature in the TXU system.

Of course, it is now fruitless to discuss what might have been had we gone back to Cleveland but there are times when it rears its head and I just put it aside. Since my brother Tom died in 1967 and was no longer a factor in the hierarchy of Process Machine I thought long and hard about calling Lee at that time to feel his pulse about my coming back but, again, I did not.

WHERE DID THE EPISCOPALIANS COME FROM

Explaining how our family became associated with the Episcopal Church and the Anglican Communion is a story that has to be told just to keep the facts straight. But in order to do so I have to talk about our very good friends Edward and Ren Veigel who lived in McKinney, Collin County, Texas, where Ed practiced law for more than 50 years until his death in August of 2003.

Ed and I grew up in the Roman Catholic Church. His family home for most of his life was in St. Paul, Minnesota. He was a navigator on a B-17 crew during WWII and was for a time stationed in San Marcus, Texas. He met Ren Hill on a blind date and married her about a year later. Ren grew up in the Presbyterian Church and so after their marriage they decided they had to do something about getting their family into the same church. How it happened I do not know but they did receive instruction in the Episcopal Church and very soon after their marriage they became members by reception and confirmation.

As I said earlier I grew up in the Roman Catholic Church and Billie grew up in the Methodist Church. We were married in 1945 in the First Methodist Church in Wichita Falls, Texas, and until August 1959 attended the Methodist Church regularly as a family and supported it with our talent and treasure although I never became a member as such. From the time we met Ed and Ren in the fall of 1946 in Austin, Texas, we talked at various times about how we should get together in the same church as a family but did nothing about it. Late in August of 1959, Ed invited me to

REN & EDWARD VEIGEL WITH DAUGHTER SANDY IN 1947

attend a Bishop Mason retreat over the Labor Day weekend at Camp Crucis near Granbury, Texas, with him and another friend, Dwayne Howell, from McKinney. Camp Crucis was a retreat center then owned by the Episcopal Diocese of Dallas and Bishop Mason was the Diocesan Bishop at that time. The camp was a rather rough affair with one building used as a dining hall and a conference room when the weather required indoor activities. Sleeping accommodations consisted of cots and bunk beds in old army surplus 4-man hut which were weather proof and adequate.

In a weak moment I agreed to go and we made plans accordingly. At the same time the wives of the participants from McKinney invited my family to visit with them over that same weekend. The format of the retreat weekend was such that after the start of the retreat there was to be no conversation with your fellow participants except at specific times during the day. The remainder of the weekend was spent in short meditations presented by the Bishop and others which were followed by short quiet times during which we were to contemplate on what had been said in the meditation periods, or we could read material which might expand on what had been said. This went on for the entire time from Saturday about 10:00 am until Noon on Monday when we left to return to our homes.

I did not know that during the time I was at Camp Crucis, Billie was given an opportunity to hear the story about the Episcopal Church from Ed and Dwayne's wives who were for the most part "converts". When I arrived home that Monday afternoon I discovered we had had a postcard inviting us to attend St. George's Episcopal Church (located on South Beckley in Dallas) to attend a new *"Inquirers Class"* the following Sunday. The Rector was a nice fellow by the name of The Reverend Frank E. Jarrett. We went to the church service the following Sunday and were so taken by what we found in the Episcopal Church that we have not been elsewhere except to visit since. We subsequently attended his weekly inquirers class for nine months. Billie was confirmed and I was received from the Roman Catholic Church in the fall of 1959 by The Rt. Rev. C. Avery Mason, the Bishop of the Diocese of Dallas. Richard and Mary Jane Groene were our sponsors.

Richard Groene and I later served on the Vestry of St. Georges just before we moved to Sherman, Grayson County, Texas. Also, while at St. George's, I served as an adult acolyte at a mid-week 5:30 am Holy Eucharist. While I was on the Vestry, Frank Jarrett resigned to take a teaching position at Trinity College in San Antonio. He also divorced his wife of many years. The Vestry called the associate minister The Rev. John C. Worrell as Rector.

My mother died of lung cancer in June 1960 and Billie's mother died in October 1960. In July 1962 we moved to Sherman, Texas, and we immediately transferred our letter to St. Stephen's Episcopal Church with The Rev. William Tate Young as Rector. Mrs. Young had died just a year or two before we arrived on the scene and Father Young was having quite a time adjusting to the loss.

Father Young was a very conservative southern gentleman and a conservative churchman. We had not been in Sherman very long when I was elected to the Vestry and then elected Junior Warden. The members of St. Stephen's were quite a mixture of very young and very old Episcopalians. The young ones were mostly air force families stationed at Perrin AFB. They had young children and were interested in having an active Sunday School Program. The oldsters, whose families were all grown and gone from home, were not too interested in spending much for expansion of the educational program. The Rector did not want to pit one group against the other so nothing more was said about the situation; however, George & Marion Midgley, and Billie and I and some others whom I cannot now recall decided that the classrooms in which we had Sunday-School needed to be painted so we repainted them. Needless to say many of the old-timers in the Parish were somewhat perturbed. As Junior Warden I decided not to pursue any new projects even if asked to do so.

In August of 1965 I was transferred back to the Dallas office of TP&L so we decided to settle in Richardson, Dallas County, Texas. In looking for a church we could not find a church in Richardson that suited us so we looked in North Dallas and found The Episcopal Church of the Transfiguration which seemed to suit our needs. We transferred our letter from St. Stephens in Sherman to the "FIG" on 13 January 1966 and stayed there until about 1994 when the liberal homosexual-loving group took over. I transferred to St. Luke's in Dallas and Billie followed a short time later.

While at the FIG I served on the Vestry twice and was on the Vestry which built the present church structure located at 14115 Hillcrest Road. I was on the Calling Committee and the Vestry which called The Rev. Terence C. Roper as Rector in May 1976 to succeed The Rev. James J. Niles who resigned to move to Dalhart.

As things stood by January 1992 we were not too happy with the change in attitude about homosexuals. It seemed to me that the Rector was trying to move the Parish in the direction that would support a national church position for the ordination of practicing homosexuals and for the blessing of same sex unions. Billie and I would not support any organization that would support such absurd positions which fail the "three-legged" test -- Is it contrary to Scripture, Tradition and Reason?

On 1 November 1994 the situation at the FIG was still unresolved so we attended St. Luke's mostly but visited other churches in the area. A special convention was called for the election of a new Diocesan Bishop of

Dallas and The Reverend James Monte Stanton was elected Bishop of Dallas on the 15th ballot. Father Stanton declared himself early on in his interview with the delegates to be against the ordination of practicing homosexuals. Also, he had said, while he was against the ordination of women, he could and would work with those already in the Diocese.

At the 1994 General Convention of the Episcopal Church in Indianapolis, the House of Bishops and House of Deputies did not take any different stand on returning to the tradition of the Episcopal Church; therefore, I decided I had to transfer my membership to St. Luke's – Dallas, and Billie followed soon after.

In the Episcopal Church of the USA, a General Convention of the Church is held every three years as compared to Diocesan Conventions which are held annually. General Convention is made up of The House of Bishops and The House of Deputies and is presided over by the Presiding Bishop of the Episcopal Church. Obviously, all Bishops of the Church, including retired Bishops, make up the House of Bishops while the House of Deputies include Priests and Lay delegates elected to represent each Diocese. The 2003 General Convention of the Church confirmed and blessed the Diocesan Election to Bishop in the State of New Hampshire of a practicing homosexual priest, The Rev. Gene Robinson. This action, which had never been done before, was contrary to scripture and the practice of the Church since the time of Christ. To compound the situation further the Presiding Bishop, Frank Griswold, not only voted for the confirmation for the action of General Convention, he participated in the consecration ceremony as a Bishop of the Church.

Needless to say, since 2003 there has been an increasing turmoil in the American Church against the action and as of the time of this writing in 2006 many churches across the USA have or are planning to withdraw from the oversight of their Diocesan Bishop and the Episcopal Church, and are securing oversight from Bishops of Africa and other places within the Anglican Communion. At this time our Diocesan Bishop of Dallas, James Monte Stanton, had taken a position supporting those Clergy or Parishes who wish to withdraw from the Episcopal Church of the USA (ECUSA). The deterioration of the situation in The Episcopal Church of the USA (ECUSA) continues to decline and where it will end only God knows.

CITY BOY

A CAREER AT TEXAS POWER & LIGHT COMPANY

As mentioned earlier in this effort, I started working for TP&L on 1 September 1952 in what was then called System Planning Division of the Engineering Department. The Division Manager, newly appointed on 1 September 1952, was John Benton Robuck, a graduate of The University of Texas about 1929.

At the time we were called the System Planning Division, there existed a Planning Department headed up by George W. Beams, a vice president and Aggie friend of W.W. Lynch, then President and General Manager of TP&L. The Planning Department was responsible for acquiring new fuel contracts and securing leases on lignite deposits in our service territory. At that time TP&L was using gas as the major boiler fuel having stopped using lignite about 1941 when the East Texas gas became very plentiful and less expensive than lignite to burn; however, Mr. Lynch expected the fuel picture to change in the long run and thus started the lignite lease acquisition program early in his new "job".

To make a long story short Mr. Beams did not want any competition in the planning business so very shortly after I started working, the name of our group was changed to the System Engineering Division although we had the responsibility for planning the expansion of the generation and transmission facilities of TP&L. So much for professional jealousy although more will be written later I am sure.

My first responsibility was to help prepare system data for use in the system modeling studies we conducted at A&M at least twice a year. A&M had the only analog computer on which electrical systems such as TP&L's could be modeled and various simulations conducted. The studies at A&M usually lasted two-full weeks during which time we could make 30-40 simulations of problems on the transmission network and then devise fixes for the particular situations. Although the modeling was the best available it did not compare to that which we were doing in later years when the digital computer came into use for such work but more about that later.

TEXAS POWER & LIGHT CO.
JOE'S EMPLOYEE RECORD

As mentioned in a previous chapter, when I was hired, our offices were in the same building that the Trailways Bus Depot was in and our offices were on the sixth floor. By March 1953 we were moved to a new building at the northeast corner of Bryan and Akard Streets and just west and across Bullington Street from the Atlantic Richfield building. This new office was quite roomy but also was a big bullpen type operation where everyone was in one large office and only the Division Manager had a private office. Our office had about twelve people including two secretaries and their typewriters. To say it was not satisfactory is an understatement.

Not too long after coming over to the Fidelity Union Life Building our Planning Section inherited the responsibility for calculating relay settings for all transmission line terminals and all distribution feeders on the system. This work had formerly been done in the Operating Department under the Relay Superintendent but was transferred to us because at the time lack of personnel had put them very far behind in the *relay-coordinations* for the system. So far behind that we concentrated more than two thirds of our effort on relay-coordinations rather than on our primary mission of planning. This went on for a few months until our employee numbers could be increased and some organization given to handling the work more appropriately.

It was during this time that I had the opportunity to do a lot of relay-coordination work for which I really did not have a hankering but it had to be done. Our leader, Charles L. Wilie, during this time was a man who had formerly been Relay Superintendent and quite knowledgeable of the transmission system. At least he knew what the system hardware was like but as for the response of the system to emergencies I am not sure he had the feel that our original group of engineers had developed. In spite of all this we worked pretty well as a team and things seemed to be going along rather smoothly until about the second quarter of 1955. Our leader, Wilie, announced one day that he was going to the doctor the next morning and he would see us in a few days. Turned out that about noon the next day he was found in a diabetic coma at his home, for he had not made it to the doctor's office at all and, before the day was over, he died from complications associated with a diabetic condition about which he knew nothing. The surprising aspect of this situation is that he was a very intelligent and well read individual and not at all unaware of the hazards of untreated diabetes.

Our business seemed to get bigger and faster after this sudden loss of such a key person and we all just had to pitch in to make a go of it all.

Joseph Jurlina

About June of 1957 I was asked to transfer to the office of Lee E. Cook as an administrative assistant without title. As mentioned earlier this was a thankless job and it lasted until about April 1962 when I was asked to move into our Central Division Headquarters in Irving, Texas, in what was called our Industrial Consultants activity. A job which required us to be familiar with the business processes of our industrial and commercial customers so that we could make suggestions on how they might use our service more efficiently. That is, how to reduce their demand and energy use without impairing the quality of their products or increasing their overall costs.

By 1 July 1962 I was asked to go to Sherman, Grayson County, Texas, to take the place of the District Manager, Bob McAfee, who was about to retire. He was a man that had lived all of his life in Sherman, Grayson County, Texas, and knew about everyone in the county. I worked with him in his capacity as Manager for just a few days, but even after he retired he was around and close to the TP&L property as much as any employee on full time status. The thing which made this difficult was the fact that he had run for and had been elected to the City Council of Sherman. A position he held for at least two terms.

Fortunately, my stay in Sherman was to last only until August of 1965 when I was asked to go back to Dallas to return to the System Engineering Division to take over the Electrical Planning Section. The section I had started in and work which I really enjoyed doing because of the professionalism of the people involved both in our company and those in other companies with whom we had much contact. This transfer came at the time when the TP&L system was undergoing a tremendous growth of about 10% per year in both demand and energy which was requiring a very significant expansion of the generation capability, a comparable expansion of its bulk transmission system and along with that the addition of many distribution substations to serve all the added load. I liked to think that my expertise and familiarity with the system both from an electrical engineers standpoint and from one who had been in the field for three years did not hurt.

My return to the Dallas Office Engineering prompted me to think again about securing my State Registration as a Professional Engineer. By this

CITY BOY

time I had worked for and with other registered engineers on various projects so I proceeded to secure references and filled out the necessary paperwork with the State Board of Professional Engineers in Austin, Texas. I received my confirmation and certification from the Board that my Registration No, 24699 was approved on 20 October 1965, our son Michael's thirteenth birthday. A day we both had cause for celebration.

This last assignment lasted until the TU reorganization in early 1984 when all the planning responsibilities in the three operating companies, TP&L, DP&L and TESCO, were consolidated in the TU offices in Dallas. I was given the title Manager System Engineering Division for all the activities that remained. These included Construction Budgeting, Distribution Relay Coordinations, and a liaison function with the TU Planners to assure our President that TP&L interests were being protected. In February 1987 another reorganization of TP&L took place in which I was made Administrative Assistant to the Chief Engineer, Joe R. Thompson, formerly with TESCO. The Construction Budgeting responsibilities were absorbed by the Engineering Services Division created for this purpose and the Distribution Relaying-Coordinations were transferred to the parent TU along with other company responsibilities. In retrospect these moves were a prelude to the second reduction-of-forces move made in about four years. In June of 1987, an announcement of a retirement offer was made to go into effect on 1 July and 1 August of 1987 available to certain employees. In effect there was to be no penalty for retiring before the age of 62 and more than 82% of the eligible 1100 plus employees system wide took the offer as made, including yours truly. So, after 35 years of faithful and loyal service it became obvious that anyone in the organization could be retired, along with many more comparably experienced employees, without much of a ripple on the quality of service to customers in the near and distant future. At least that was the impression management wanted to make on employees and the public in general. Time will tell whether any of that was true.

Joseph Jurlina

BILLIE & JOSEPH JURLINA ON 31 JULY 1987 "LAST DAY ACTIVE DUTY" WITH ROBERT K. CAMPBELL, PRES. OF TP&L & PITT PITTMAN VP OF T

CAROL ANN JURLINA KRUMM & FAMILY

After moving to Dallas to begin my career with TP&L company, Carol Ann attended grade school and junior high school in Dallas before we moved to Sherman, TX in the summer of 1962 where she entered high school in the fall. While participating in the drill team, she developed a great friendship with Ann (Berthold) Mrizek who became like a second daughter in the family, and has continued to the present time to visit us (even helping us pack and move!), as well as Carol Ann & Bill. In her Senior year of high school, Carol Ann was introduced to and began to date William Evans Krumm. After HS graduation, Carol Ann attended Texas Tech University for two years, including the year that Bill was serving a tour in Viet Nam, September 1966 to September 1967. Carol Ann and Bill were married, March 9, 1968 and afterward lived in Junction City, Kansas for a year while Bill completed his U.S. Army commitment at Fort Riley, Kansas.

CITY BOY

From July 1962 through August 1965, Billie and I and the children lived in Sherman, Grayson County, Texas, while I served as TP&L Sherman District Manager. Annually, the Sherman Chamber of Commerce sponsored a fashion show and luncheon, and sometime in 1964 our daughter, Carol Ann, was asked to participate in the style show for that year. Of course, her mother and I were delighted to have her involved in such a production for all the reasons that parents wish the best for their children.

These luncheons are generally attended by Chamber members and their wives but many other guests attend also because of the popularity of the program. Lawrence H. Krumm, Councilman and Chamber member, and his wife Mae were among those present. In fact, the Krumms and the Jurlinas sat at the same table along with others.

During the course of the style show, after Carol Ann had made a couple of appearances in different dresses, Larry Krumm leaned over and said in a subdued voice "dare I introduce your daughter to our son Bill?" Subsequently, Bill and Carol Ann had a "coke date" and the rest is history.

Carol Ann was in her third year at Texas Tech University majoring in dietetics through the Home Economics Department. Bill had just returned from service in Vietnam and had another year or so to serve in the Army. They had corresponded almost every day while he was overseas. Upon his return, they decided to marry and set the date for 9 March 1968. The wedding was at our church - The Episcopal Church of the Transfiguration located at 14115 Hillcrest Road in Dallas, Dallas County, Texas. At the time of their marriage, The Reverend James J. Niles was rector of the parish and they were married in what then was the Parish Hall. Our son Michael Kenneth served as acolyte during the wedding to assist the rector and The Reverend William Ketchum.

After Bill was released from his military obligation at Fort Riley at Junction City, Kansas they moved to Denton, Denton County, Texas, where they both enrolled in North Texas State University to complete their college work. As soon as Carol Ann completed her course work at North Texas State University (NTSU) she began her dietetic internship at Parkland Hospital. She completed this work and then fulfilled other obligations to become a registered dietician and a member of the American Dietetic Association (ADA). Carol Ann worked at Presbyterian & Baylor Hospitals before moving into consulting. She consulted part-time for several years at Dallas Home for the Jewish Aged while their children were in school. 24 years at Baylor University Medical Center in various RD positions, both inpatient and outpatient--the last 15 years as a Certified Diabetes Educator, before retiring in March 2013. (Pictured with Joel Allison, CEO of Baylor as she received her 20 year pin.)

Bill completed his work in the Business School at NTSU and began his career in 1971 with Henry S. Miller Company in Dallas, TX. Within two years of moving back to the Dallas area, Bill and Carol Ann purchased a lot in Richardson, Dallas County, Texas, at #5 Waterview Place and designed and built their home. Their cul-de-sac lot is backed by a creek was an ideal location to raise their family. They were only two miles from us and about an hour from Bill's folks who still resided in Sherman. During Bill's career in finance he has worked for several prominent commercial lending organizations and even ventured into business for himself twice.

Joseph Jurlina

JASON WILLIAM AND KATHERINE ALLISON KRUMM

Jason William Krumm, our first grandchild, was born at 9:10 a.m. on 30 June 1973 in Presbyterian Hospital located at 8200 Walnut Hill Lane in Dallas, Dallas County, Texas. Jason weighed in at seven pounds twelve and one half ounces and had blonde hair and "blue" eyes.

Our first grandchild probably was spoiled as much as other first grandchildren are by proud grandparents. The first picture of Jason, made by Grandmother Jurlina within the first two hours of his life in the hospital, was the first of many to be made in subsequent years by very proud grandparents.

Jason William was baptized by The Rev. Virgil Meyer at the 10:45 a.m. service on 26 August 1973 at Messiah Lutheran Church in Richardson, Dallas County, Texas. His sponsors were his Uncle and Aunt, Mr. & Mrs. Larry H. Krumm, Jr. who lived in Tyler, Smith County, TX. Jason was also confirmed at Messiah Lutheran Church on 12 April 1987 by The Rev. Virgil Meyer. Jason William Krumm was graduated from J.J. Pearce High School in Richardson, Texas, on 2 June 1991. He attended A&M University for one semester but was not ready to make the commitment to study. After

CITY BOY

laying out of school for a short time he attended Junior College at the Richland and Brookhaven campuses where he made the Dean's list. In the fall of 1994 he enrolled at the University of Texas at Austin planning to get into the UT School of Architecture and subsequently received his Bachelor of Architecture in May of 1999. His first assignment after graduation was in the Dallas area with Corgan architectural firm which was involved in expansion of DFW airport. He then moved to Minneapolis, Minnesota for a three-year stay with Msada, a firm concerned with church, school, and medical construction in developing nations. Jason was then employed by the commercial firm, Newman Architecture, in Naperville, Illinois for two years before transferring to their non-profit organization, Schools for the Children of the World. After several months of designing and preparing drawings and exploratory trips, he moved to Léogâne, Haiti. He is presently the project manager overseeing the construction of schools being rebuilt following the destructive earthquake in January 2010. How could we have known, while on our celebratory family cruise in the western Carribean Sea (more on that later), that the earthquake of which we were alerted, would become the next focus for Jason's service? Since May of 2013 we have been blessed to have him take a sabbatical in Dallas after completing his contract in Haiti and hope he will make it more permanent.

His sister, Katherine Allison Krumm, was born at 3:00 p.m. on 18 June 1976 in Presbyterian Hospital located at 8200 Walnut Hill Lane in Dallas, Dallas County, Texas. Katherine weighed in at eight pounds six and one half ounces and was twenty inches long. She was born with black hair and "blue" eyes.

CITY BOY

Katherine is our second grandchild and our first granddaughter. She was baptized on 1 August 1976 at Messiah Lutheran Church by The Rev. Virgil Meyer. Her sponsors were her Uncle and Aunt, Mr. & Mrs. Larry H. Krumm, Jr. who live in Tyler, Smith County, Texas. Katherine was also confirmed at Messiah on 8 April 1990 by The Rev. Michael Harding.

She was graduated from J.J. Pearce High School in May of 1993 and enrolled at Concordia Lutheran College in Austin, Texas. She was active in school and church choirs and took voice and piano lessons. Her ultimate goal was to teach. After attending Concordia Lutheran College in Austin she went on to Concordia in Minneapolis, MN to complete her BA degree in Elementary Education. She then went to Wheaton College in Wheaton, Illinois to complete her MA degree in Educational Ministries with an emphasis in spiritual formation and discipleship.

While attending college in St. Paul, MN Katherine met Ryan Michael Clark, pre-seminarian of the Lutheran Church Missouri Synod. Katherine and Ryan were married on 6 June 1998 in Richardson, Texas at Messiah Lutheran Church with Dennis Bohren, Ryan's childhood pastor and mentor, officiating. The wedding was one of the most beautiful ceremonies we ever attended and I am certain it was so for me just because it was our beautiful granddaughter being married.

KATHERINE KRUMM/RYAN CLARK WEDDING – 6 JUNE 1998

Joseph Jurlina

Hope Katherine Clark, their first child, was born on 21 early in 2000 in St. Louis, St. Louis County, Missouri at St. Mary's Hospital during Ryan's second year of seminary requirements. They moved to Seymour, Jackson County, Indiana for Ryan to complete his Vicarage from July 2000 until July 2001. Their second child, Anastasia Noelle, was born on shortly after Christmas in 2002 back in St. Louis, Missouri, also at St. Mary's Hospital, during the final of four years of seminary. Ryan Michael Clark graduated with his Master's of Divinity in May of 2002 and was ordained the following month as clergyman in the Lutheran Church, Missouri Synod. The ordination took place in his home church, Christ the King Lutheran church, in Spencer, Iowa. During the same month they moved to Wisconsin Rapids, Wood County, Wisconsin where Ryan began serving his first call as associate pastor at St. Luke's Lutheran Church. Josiah Michael Clark, their third child, was born on 8 December of 2004 in Marshfield, WI at St. Joseph's Hospital. In March 2006 they moved to Walden, Orange County, New York. Joshua Ryan Clark their second son was born in the spring of 2007 in Newburgh, New York at St. Luke's Hospital. Ryan has now been in the pastoral ministry for eleven years and serves as the Senior Pastor at Trinity Evangelical Lutheran Church. Katherine homeschools their four children and teaches Bible study at church.

151

CITY BOY

HOPE & JOSIAH CLARK, GREAT GRANDFATHER JOSEPH & ANYA

MICHAEL KENNETH JURLINA AND FAMILY

When we moved back to Dallas in 1965 to Richardson, TX, Mike attended Richardson High School (where Billie later taught Home Economics for several years). Before graduating in 1971 Mike had the opportunity to sing bass in the RHS choir which recorded great Christmas albums, both of which are long-time family favorites.

Joseph Jurlina

After attending one semester at Baylor University in Waco, TX where he was not enamored with college, he joined the U.S. Army in 1972, serving in the "Old Guard"(1st Battalion Presidential Guard) in Washington, D.C.

JOSEPH & MICHAEL – CHISTMAS 1969

WO-2 MICHAEL JURLINA IN GERMANY – 1976

MICHAEL KENNETH JURLINA IN WASHINGTON, DC "OLD GUARD" IN 1973

After being accepted for flight school, he completed U. S. Army Helicopter Flight School training (as part of the last class to go through Fort Wolters) in Mineral Wells, TX , August, 1973, and subsequently served in Germany where Billie and Joe spent an enjoyable Christmas with him in 1976. After his discharge from the army, he contracted as an instructor in rotary wing instrument flight training at Fort Rucker, Alabama—"home of Army Aviation", and while there, earned his own Fixed Wing License/Certification.

153

Upon his return to Dallas, Mike flew for a private company, Colhmia; then flew helicopters for Pumpkin Air. After finishing his jet training and flying for corporate employers, he succeeded in obtaining employment with American Airlines, eventually becoming Captain on the 777, and became a Check Airman for the 777 fleet, as well as other accomplishments.

MICHAEL KENNETH JURLINA & PAMELA ELAINE HASTY
WEDDING ON 10 MAY 1986 IN DALLAS, TX

Michael Kenneth Jurlina and Pamela Elaine Hasty were married on 10 May 1986 in The Episcopal Church of the Transfiguration located at 14115 Hillcrest Road in Dallas, Dallas County, Texas, with The Reverend Terence C. Roper, Rector, officiating.

At the time of their marriage Michael was, and continues to this day, flying for American Airlines, arm of AMR Corporation, while Pamela was a registered nurse at the Medical City Hospital - Dallas located at 7777 Forest Lane in Dallas, Dallas County, Dallas. Pamela was the coordinator of pre-natal education for prospective parents at the time of their marriage. Today (2010) she is a Diabetes Educator at Plano, Collin County, Texas.

Pam and Michael met while Michael was a patient at Medical City about 1981. Pamela was the lovely nurse on duty for the first shift the day that Mike was admitted. The rest is history. After their union, their family grew with the birth of Jacob Jarrett Jurlina mid-summer 1987, and then again when Sabrina Nicole Jurlina was born during the winter of 1991. Since we were recently retired and lived relatively close to Mike and Pam, we enjoyed being able to babysit and frequently attend Jacob and Sabrina's school activities.

In April 1992 Michael and Pamela along with their children son Jacob Jarrett and Sabrina Nicole Jurlina lived in their home located at 2501 Belmont Place, Plano, Collin County, Texas, 75023. However, they sold their home and moved into a rental home in Plano until their new home was designed and constructed at 7023 Winding Creek Road in Dallas, TX. The waiting period was expected to be about six or seven months but lasted about twelve months. Their home is a spacious, two-story Austin stone located only a few miles north of where we live. It has been a joy for our whole family to celebrate birthdays and other special occasions together at their home.

CITY BOY

JACOB JARRETT AND SABRINA NICOLE JURLINA

Jacob Jarrett Jurlina was born after a long day of waiting at 10:52 p.m. on 13 July 1987 at Medical City Hospital in Dallas, Dallas County, Texas. He weighed in at eight pounds five and one half ounces and was twenty one and one half inches long. He was born with brown hair and "blue" eyes.

Joseph Jurlina

Present at the hospital at the time of Jacob's arrival in addition to Michael, the father, were: Joseph and Billie Jurlina the proud paternal grandparents; William E. and Carol Ann Jurlina Krumm, the Uncle and Aunt of Jacob; Jason William and Katherine Allison Krumm, cousins of Jacob; Jerri & Michael Peiffer, aunt and uncle; and Marilyn Calfee, maternal grandmother.

Jacob was baptized on All Saints Day 1987 at The Church of the Transfiguration-Dallas Episcopal Church located at 14115 Hillcrest Road in Dallas, Dallas County, Texas, with the Reverend Terence C. Roper, Rector, officiating. Jacob's sponsors were his aunt and uncle, Mr. & Mrs. Michael L. Peiffer.

JOSEPH AND JACOB JURLINA – 19 JANUARY 2003

Jacob is our third grandchild and therefore his Jurlina grandparents have had a considerable amount of practice spoiling grandchildren. Although grandmother is Jacob's favorite grandparent in Dallas, grandfather has had ample time to try his hand at "spoiling" him also. Jacob attended our church Parish Day School starting in kindergarten though the sixth grade. He completed his seventh year through High School at St. Mark's Dallas private school for boys having graduated in 2005. While at St. Mark's he was a member of a great Ice Hockey Team. He graduated from the Cox

CITY BOY

Business School at Southern Methodist University under scholastic scholarship on 15 May 2010 with a Bachelor's degree in Business Administration. He had a summer internship in 2008 in Houston, Texas with J. P. Morgan Company. Following graduation, he moved to Houston, TX, the heart of the oil industry, where he worked for EP Energy. Still in Houston, Jacob works for Rothschild, a European Investment Bank.

Jacob's little sister, Sabrina Nicole Jurlina, was born at 11:41 a.m. on 15 February 1991, the day following St. Valentine's Day, in Medical City Hospital located at 7777 Forest Lane in Dallas, Dallas County, Texas. She weighed eight pounds eight ounces and was twenty one and one quarter inches long, and had brown hair and "blue" eyes. Before her birth Jacob and his mother while reviewing a list of names for the new daughter came upon the name Sabrina. When Jacob heard Sabrina, enjoying the rhyme with Jurlina, exclaimed "That's It!".

Joseph Jurlina

Her "Big" brother Jacob Jarrett was very excited about his new sister and is very protective of her.

Present in the hospital very shortly after Sabrina's birth, in addition to the proud father Michael Kenneth, were Billie and Joseph Jurlina, her paternal grandparents; Mrs. Marilyn Calfee, her maternal grandmother; Carol Ann Jurlina Krumm and husband William E. Krumm, Aunt and Uncle of Sabrina. Jason William and Katherine Allison Krumm, cousins, were in school and came to visit later in the afternoon.

MICHAEL, PAMELA JURLINA WITH CHILDREN JACOB & SABRINA
1992

One of the more significant events which occurred at the hospital after Sabrina's arrival was the delivery of a helium-inflated balloon, about 30 inches in diameter, supporting a basket of flowers. This was a gift with well wishes from Dr. & Mrs. Robert and Michelle Kauffman, a doctor who had a medical practice in the Medical City Complex, and who is a vestryman in The Church of the Transfiguration, the Church of the Jurlinas.

Sabrina Nicole was baptized on 19 May 1991 at The Church Of The Transfiguration-Episcopal located at 14115 Hillcrest Road in Dallas, Dallas County, Texas 75240, The Reverend Trawin E. Malone officiating. Sabrina's sponsors were also Mr. & Mrs. Michael L. Peiffer, her mother's sister, Jerri, and her husband. Sabrina was a happy baby as was her brother. She has a unique personality just as do the rest of us. She loves music and started taking piano lessons at about the age of three.

Sabrina attended the Parish Episcopal School, as did her brother, starting in Kindergarten, and completed her studies through high school there graduating in 2009. She has also been very active in her church and has been on mission trips to Belize. She has sung and played piano at school and for the Contemporary Services at her church. At Parish Episcopal School she was involved in volleyball, basketball and track. She was Co-

JACOB & SISTER SABRINA JURLINA

Captain of the Football Cheerleaders. Her musical interests include piano and voice lessons. She excelled in piano to the point that she was awarded the second place in the state of Texas. After graduation from High School she visited several University campuses but settled on Texas Christian University in Fort Worth, Texas where she received a very nice academic scholarship. She graduated from TCU in May 2013 with a business degree and music minor. She is also pursuing a modeling career which led her to Greece and Germany for the summer of 2012 and Sydney, Australia for the fall of 2013.

Billie and I are so very fortunate to have four lovely, loving grandchildren and four very young and lovely great grandchildren to enjoy in our senior years. I guess it is a fact of life that families must make their livelihoods

Joseph Jurlina

where the opportunities present themselves else we would all live within a stones throw of each other. That does not keep us from praying for the time in our lives when all of our families will be within a half-days ride from home, Amen.

CITY BOY

RETIREMENT ITS CAUSES AND RESULTS

Since thirty five years of my professional life were invested with Texas Power & Light Company, an operating company within the Texas Utilities Company System, I feel very strongly about many things that have happened in the utility business in Texas these last few years. Some of them I have to talk about while some others I probably should just forget about.

Texas Utilities Company in the late seventies and early eighties was trying to complete its first venture into the nuclear generation business. That is, Comanche Peak Units #1 & #2 were involved in a very unpleasant and probably 98% unnecessary controversy started by a group of "do-gooders".

Escalating operating costs in almost all areas were the straw that forced top management to decide on some extra-ordinary force-reductions and one was made late in 1983. In that reduction, some monetary inducement was given to those eligible in equivalent salary through the end-of-year after retirement in August. Had I been two years older, when the offer was made, I probably would have considered the option to retire very seriously.

The second force-reduction was required in 1987 and was offered without penalty, as required for employees aged 55-62 under the existing retirement plan, to those employees with fifteen or more years of service over the age of fifty five. I was eligible this second time around since I was sixty-one at the time of the offering. It was obvious that the new forces in charge wanted me to accept the offer from a number of events which had occurred the previous two or three years. So, I accepted the offer, but not until several weeks had passed and not until several rumors that I planned to stay till I reached seventy years of age were planted by someone. My retirement became effective 1 August 1987 before my 62nd birthday on 19 September lacking one month being my 35th complete year of service.

As I recall, I was one of the 82% of the eligible employees that retired. Of over 1100 eligible within the operating arms of TU, almost 900 retired on 1 July and 1 August in the largest exodus of electric utility talent in the history of the business in Texas. For TP&L alone the lost experience represented over 4600 man-years of service. Needless to say, the TU Electric organization will never be the same again.

Jacob Jarrett Jurlina and his parents Michael and Pamela were present at the retirement ceremony. This was exciting in itself since much of the interest of fellow employees and families was the presence of this very young Jurlina grandchild. Remembering my date of retirement was made easy by the fact that Jacob was born on 13 July before my retirement on the first of August that same year.

LIFE AFTER RETIREMENT

THE EARLY YEARS 1987-1992

Billie retired from teaching in the Richardson Independent School District on the 1 February 1987 before I retired from my position as Administrative Assistant to the Chief Engineer of the Texas Power & Light Division of TU Electric on 1 August 1987. We both had decided that we would not make any firm plans about what other employment we might pursue for a year or so after retirement. We did agree to spend more time involved in and with our hobbies, church, genealogical research, children and grandchildren, and do some of the traveling we had talked about.

CITY BOY

To this date in November 1991, we have done all those things and are still trying to decide about re-employment, although Billie has had the opportunity to work a few hours only on a part-time basis with Cloth World. She has done that so that she could take advantage of the employee discounts when purchasing materials for her sewing. Philosophically, neither of us is ready for seriously looking for other full or even part-time employment so we will enjoy retirement as long as we can on our current income.

Billie became re-involved in the Women of the Church and the Altar Guild as well as being Historian for both the WOC and the TSPE Auxiliary. She also did more sewing for her granddaughters and herself.

Joseph returned to playing golf after practically giving up the game for about 25 years. He had been playing in two senior associations until the spring of 1991: L.B. Houston Senior Golf Association at the City of Dallas L.B. Houston course on Luna Road on Mondays, and The North Texas Senior Golf Association which played on a different course each Wednesday morning. He gave up the North Texas group because play was too slow; therefore, he now can choose the courses he wants to play with his golfing buddy Robert G. Johnson. On 5 March 1991, I was playing in a "fivesome" at L. B. Houston when on 15th hole of 151 yards I teed of first and to my amazement my tee-shot landed on the front of the hole and the ball bounced once more and finally went into the hole. None of my associates acknowledged the situation for 2-3 minutes and kept on talking as if nothing of any consequence had just occurred. In the discussion which followed, all of them admitted they had never made a hole-in-one nor had any of them ever witnessed such an event.

In recent years (2009) my participation in golf tournaments has been restricted to being the "designated putter".

I had also been entering Billie's VICK-FAMILY genealogical data in a data base called Personal Ancestral File (PAF) by the Mormons. The Joseph Vick Family of America, Inc. was organized and incorporated in North Carolina in 1991 after having met informally for about 10 years. We went to all but one reunion between 1985 and 1991 in Mississippi and Virginia. Billie was one of eight board members in the organization.

Joseph Jurlina

I also tried to gather JURLINA-FAMILY data but with more difficulty because most of the ancestors are in Jugoslavia. In the last twelve months (2006) or so, however, I made contact with a first cousin in Zadar, Jugoslavia, and a second or third cousin in Sasolburg, South Africa. All these in addition to some JURLINAS in Pennsylvania, Ohio, British Columbia, New Jersey, New York, and Australia. The families all seem to originate in Seline, Jugoslavia, but the ties between all the families have not yet been established for certain. Much of the work on the Cleveland side of the family has been done by William George Avenmarg, a cousin, in Parma, Ohio, who has copyrighted some material provided for my PAF data base.

One thing that changed drastically post-retirement was having and using the free time to play golf. Robert G. Johnson and his wife Dorace were very much into ballroom dancing at Union Station with us when it was going full swing. He retired from Dillard's about the time I retired and took up golf rather seriously. He has also been my golf partner since 1987 along with Bobbie Pair who lived in Rockwall, Texas, with his wife Edith.

Bobbie was a fireman with the Atlanta, Georgia, Fire Department for years until his retirement in 1987. He was a better golfer than Bob Johnson and myself and beat us pretty regularly. Unfortunately, Bobbie was a 2-3 pack-a-day cigarette smoker for 30 plus years, and only gave up the habit about the time he retired. In February of 1990 he developed some soreness and swelling in his lymph glands of his neck. After some tests and x-rays he was diagnosed with adeno-carcinoma of the esophagus and much involvement in the lymph system. He received chemotherapy for several months but to no avail and he died rather suddenly one week-end with pneumonia or a failure of his respiratory system. The game has not been the same for me since Bobbie Pair died.

The week before Easter in 1992, Bob and Dorace Johnson moved to Hot Springs Village in northwestern Arkansas. They leased a house to determine for certain that they really want to live in Hot Springs Village where golf is the most important thing to do. We all hope they have made the right decision about the move. I continued to play golf with Syd Terry and Dale Simpson at Tennison at least once a week.

CITY BOY

THE YEARS AFTER 1992

My golf activities dwindled from 2-3 times per week to 1-2 times per year. All this as a result of all my buddies moving off, the onset of Osteo-arthritis in my major knee and hip-joints, and my lower-back-problems in my aging body, ha. Three of my golfing buddies have moved out of Texas so it is easy to just quit the game which continues to get harder to enjoy.

Our genealogical research efforts also came to a screeching halt for a couple of reasons. First, my response to my Cousin Tome Jurlina, from Belgrade, Serbia who had sent us a bunch of data about the Jurlinas of Seline, Croatia was not forthcoming. Second, it was easier to "get busy" doing other things at home, in Church, or at the YMCA.

I met a fellow on the Internet by the name of Anthony Buchic who lives in Valparaiso, Indiana who happens to have quite a bit of information about the Jurlinas who married into the Buchic family back in Croatia. In the spring of 2001 he told me he was to visit Croatia again and would be in Seline, Croatia, my Dad's birthplace, sometime that summer. As it turned out he was boarding a plane in Zagreb for a return flight to Indiana the same day (2001) we arrived in Zagreb. Later that year he sent me a listing of births and marriages of Jurlinas in Seline dating back to about 1825. It had more and better information about our Jurlina clan than I had acquired at that time. His name and address follow: Anthony C. Buchic; 56 Green Acres Drive; Valparaiso, IN 46383-1845; phone number 219-462-1271; e-mail = tcbuchic@earthlink.net   I later had communication from Cousin Tomo of Belgrade. He published a book about the Jurlinas of Croatia named SELO SELINE PLEME JURLINA, loosely translated FROM THE COMMUNITY OF SELO TO THE COMMUNITY OF SELINE, THE FAMILY JURLINA. The book and all communications from Cousin Tomo are written in Serbo-Croatian of which I have very little knowledge. For that reason I have not been able to decipher all the information about individual family members other than birth, death and such dates.

Joseph Jurlina

PEOPLE, NON-FAMILY, WHO MADE A DIFFERENCE

Leonard Byron- I first met Mr. Leonard Byron about 1955 when, as I recall, he came back to work for TP&L. His responsibility included the then called *Operating Department*, that included all transmission, distribution, and generation facilities. I am not certain when he became Vice President but he found me in 1957 when I was moved to Mr. Lee E. Cook's office as an Engineer or aide.

During the summer of 1957, TP&L was actively involved in the National Civil Defense activities. As an electrical utility, TP&L was asked to appoint a representative from the Company to the Texas State Civil Defense Committee. The Committee members participated in CD activities that included the preparation of assumed nuclear radiation-patterns over our facilities during CD exercises. During the first two meetings of this Committee, Gene Wawak and I represented our Company. Mr. Byron took an active roll in the discussions of CD involvement and was very supportive of our work.

From 1957 through 1962, while in Mr. Cook's office, I represented Mr. Cook when he was not available for the monthly meetings with the Operating Personnel at the ALCOA Plant located at Rockdale, Texas. It was during the long drives to and from Rockdale that I had the opportunity to get to know Mr. Byron very well. As compared to other officers in the TP&L organization, Mr. Byron impressed me as the ideal manager and executive, one I would expect to find in a large company. I did not hesitate to approach him with any company or personal problems because he was the best father-figure I had ever known.

Some years later Mr. Byron was given responsibility for all Divisional Operations overseeing the Districts in our service territory. It was at this point I went to Mr. Byron and asked him if he could find a place in the Divisional Operations for a hard-working engineer. He agreed that I needed to move on in my career and he would look for a situation. Early in 1962, Mr. Byron approached me about moving into, what at that time was, the Central Division Office located in Irving, Texas. Specifically, he wanted me to become acquainted with the District and Divisional problems. He made no promises about the future but it was obvious to me he was giving me an opportunity to prove myself outside of the Dallas General Office. I was delighted with the offer and I am sure at this point Mr. Cook was more excited than I because his responsibilities had been reduced somewhat and he could no longer justify having an assistant. The rest of this story is covered in detail in an earlier chapter dealing with my career at TP&L.

Sister Mary Athenasia- As mentioned elsewhere in these epistles, I was enrolled in a Roman Catholic parochial school for the first eight-years of my formal education. The school was St. Vitus located next door to the church on Glass Avenue between 61st and Norwood Road in Cleveland, Cuyahoga County, Ohio.

My first and third grade teacher as I now recall was Sister Athenasia, a nun in the order of Sisters of Notre Dame, to whom I give full credit for my reading and writing ability or lack thereof. She was without a doubt the best thing that happened to me in elementary school because she was the most diligent and patient teacher with all the children. She was obviously very proud of her students and their accomplishments and made it a point to follow their progress through the rest of their stay at St. Vitus.

Sister Mary Frumenza- As I now recall Sister Mary Frumenza was my instructor in the sixth, seventh and eight grades. I cannot now recall any other sisters in my life at St. Vitus. Sister Frumenza was a little older than all the other nuns in the school and as I now recall she was also the nun-in-charge in the school. At least that is the impression I came away with. Of course, remembering that I was only thirteen when I left St. Vitus, my facts may not be too reliable, but impressions last a long time whether true or not.

Sister Frumenza was a task master but she made it fun, and so even the boys enjoyed her methods of extracting all kinds of extra work out of us. She was not much of an artist but she recognized the ability of her students and used that ability to its fullest.

Joseph Jurlina

In our classrooms the front wall had a blackboard made up of five slates and the center slate was always reserved for some sort of scene done with colored chalk by one of the students, usually Albert Vidmar who, although color-blind, was quite an artist. I generally picked the colors for him so that it ended up being a joint project of sorts and that did not do my ego any harm.

Sister Frumenza did not tolerate any horseplay or distractions in her classes and therefore I was in trouble a good bit of the time. My cousin Josephine Bizil sat in front of me oftentimes because we were seated by height in the classrooms with the tallest at the back of the room. Our being farthest away from the teacher did not help for I was forever dipping my cousin's hair in the open ink-wells we had. Invariably I was caught in the act and it was 5-6 swats with a ruler across the back of the hand or a long chat about behavior in the cloakroom.

ALBERT JAMES VIDMAR & JOSEPH JURLINA ABT FALL 1942

Albert James Anthony Vidmar- Albert Vidmar was a neighbor of mine who lived on the South side of Carl Avenue just around the corner and about three homes East from our home on 63rd Street. He was always shorter and smaller than I was but we were always the best of friends. Our friendship covered the period from the first grade though high school at East Technical High where we both took the College Preparatory Option along with the Electrical Shop Specialty offered by the vocational school at that time.

As I mentioned previously, Al had quite an artistic bent and I always expected him to be an architect, commercial artist or cartoonist; however, he too majored in Electrical Engineering, having received his Bachelor of Science and, I believe, his Master of Science Degrees from what was then Case Institute of Technology. Case, has since been consolidated with Western Reserve University and is now Case-Western Reserve University I believe.

Al and I were almost inseparable all of our growing up days though high school. Upon graduation from East Technical H.S. in June 1942 we both went to work for Cleveland Electric Illuminating Company, CEI, in the Service Department and both ended up repairing and testing old GE Model I-14, 5-Ampere kiloWatt-hour meters which were in turn sold to several South American countries and Mexico.

I was drafted into the Army of the United States in February of 1943 but, as I recall Al stayed at CEI for a while longer and went on to Case either in night school or as a full time student.

One incident which occurred between Al and me may be worth recording at this juncture while I am reminiscing. It was a cold winter day when we were about 10-12 and were "out in the street horsing around". As boys are wont to do we were doing our usual and Al took my knitted hat away from me and started to run away with it. As I said earlier, I was enough taller than Al that I could generally outrun him in any lengthy race. In this case, we were running down the street-side of Carl Ave, just around the corner from home at 1157 East 63rd Street and I was about to overtake him to recover my hat when he stopped and "hunkered" down. Traveling at top speed I could not stop so I toppled over him head-first and my head struck the curb with the full force of my body behind me. I can remember being helped up by Al and taken home, and then being nauseous for several days. My mother later told me I did not keep any food down for almost a week and was incoherent a part of the time. To my knowledge no medical attention was sought and I finally recovered.

Joseph Jurlina

Al was the youngest in a larger family than ours. His brother Tony was the tallest in the family, about 6'-4", and quite a baseball player. While playing "softball" on the East Madison public school playground he loved to play center field because it gave him the opportunity to demonstrate his agility jumping the four-foot wrought iron fence in deep center field while trying to catch the long fly balls. More often than not he was successful at the attempts and was quite impressive to those of us that were much younger but impressionable. Needless to say we talked about the feat but never tried to emulate this "brave action".

Al died of some sort of cancer in 1988 about a month before Billie and I went to Cleveland to participate in the 50th anniversary of our 8th grade class graduation. Al's widow and a young son were there to represent Al because he had been looking forward to being present for the occasion.

Andrew L. Truden- Andrew L. Truden was a boy about four years older than I who lost his parents, I believe, in an automobile-train accident in Cleveland. He had one brother, Frank and two sisters who to my recollection were all older than Andrew. The brother was in college and old enough to be appointed guardian of Andrew and the remaining family. This family lived together in a home located behind the little one-time saloon just across the street from our home on 63rd Street. The oldest sister was out of high school and employed but Andrew and one sister were still in school.

To this day I do not know why this boy and his brother and sisters befriended me but they did. I was permitted to visit in their home, especially during the winter when there was not much to do outdoors. Andrew and I, if you can imagine 10-14 year-olds being this quiet and gentile, would sit down and for hours at a time read textbooks that the older brother had used in college. It was in their home that I first read about the Russian Revolution and stories about how the peasants were run down in the streets of Moscow by the Cossacks of the Czarist Rulers.

This close relationship did not last more than a year because the Trudens had to find larger quarters for the family and they moved far enough away that I lost all contact with them.

CITY BOY

I believe that this family with the "big brother and sister" had a very pronounced effect on my quieting down and becoming more of a student than I might have been. As I recall, one other reason for moving from the neighborhood was to get away from the influence of the drinking and fighting that took place on weekends especially among some of the families in the area.

On 27 April 2010 I decided to try to find Andrew, if he were still living, so I looked for the white pages on the Internet for Ohio and Indiana. To my surprise I found an Andrew L. Truden listed in Zionsville, Indiana at 1340 Hickory Street and his phone number is 317-733-9080 so I called him. Sure enough and to my surprise it was the Andrew that I had known back in Cleveland at least 75 years ago. He is 89 years old and lives in a retirement home with his 82 year old wife Jean who had a stroke a year or so ago. They live about 20 miles from Indianapolis. He was reminded about an incident that took place 40 or more years ago. It seems that he and his wife were at the Indianapolis 500 enjoying the race. They stopped for lunch at an outdoor spot and two motorcyclists drove up and were seated next to Andy. In a short time after all four people had been conversing, one of the cyclists leaned over and asked "did you attend St. Vitus School in Cleveland, Ohio"? Andy and his wife had not mentioned being from Cleveland or being of Slovenian extraction. This was the high light of our conversation. The name TRUDEN means tired. .

John J. Misic- John J. Misic was about 3-4 years older than I and quite interested in amateur radio and things electrical. John was already in high school when I first started going to his workshop to watch and help in the construction projects John had going on all the time. He too enrolled in the Electrical Shop Specialty program at Tech and was also a part-time employee running the school Meter-Tool Shop for the night school classes conducted at Tech.

It was John that received his Amateur Radio License W8VRJ from the FCC in 1941 and completed his first transceiver late the night of 6 December 1941, too late to get on the air for the first time. He planned to use his new equipment on Sunday, 7 December 1941, but before he had an opportunity to transmit, news of the Japanese bombing of Pearl Harbor and the subsequent Declaration of War by the Congress was announced.

Joseph Jurlina

The FCC regulations during war time stopped him from using the equipment until the end of hostilities.

John enlisted in the Marine Corp to avoid being drafted and started his boot camp in North Carolina I believe at Camp LeJuene or Cherry Point. He moved around the South Pacific Theater involved in the radar installations there and ended up on Okinawa.

Both of John's parents were born in the Slovenian part of Austria, if my memory serves me right. The senior Misic worked for Willard Storage Battery people for a long time as a welder. The work was dirty but paid well and Mr. Misic worked many long hours.

John's family was the first on our block to buy a new car in 1941. As I recall only one other family, the Dolenc's, owned a used car. The new Misic car was a 1941 Plymouth with every option available at that time for a total cost of less than $900. John was the only driver in the family so, when war was declared and John left home to go into the Marines early in 1942, the car was put up on blocks and never driven again until John was discharged from the Marine Corp sometime in 1945 or 1946.

John, too, had gone to work for CEI upon graduation from High School and when the war was over returned to CEI. When he retired, John was Vice President in charge of Operations and Construction of CEI. John and his second wife Ann came to Dallas to visit us in 1990 while on his first driving trip through Texas and the southwest. John's first wife and mother of one son died as a result of multiple sclerosis some years ago. The Misics now live at 37370 Windy Hill Lane. in Solon, Ohio, 44139, and their telephone number is 216-248-7099. John's second wife died about 1998.

John had one brother Bill who was quite a baseball player and a good friend and classmate of my brother Robert S. Jurlina all through school. Bill and my brother Bob should have played baseball with the Cleveland Indians but their careers were affected by the Korean War and the need to serve time in the service of the USA.

Helmut Wagner- Mr. Helmut Wagner was my Instructor at East Technical H.S. during my senior year in the Electrical Specialty program. He was a fine person and a graduate electrical engineer who tried to influence those of us in his class to study hard and to go on with our studies as long as we could. I am sure he knew many of us could not go on to college because of the economic conditions which prevailed at the time (1939-1942), nevertheless he involved us in experiments of induction heating, for example, that were designed to peak our interest and make us ask questions about the theoretical aspects involved.

Mr. Wagner was frail and obviously not a healthy person, for it seemed he always had a cough, much like that of my mother who finally died from adeno-carcinoma of the lungs. I do not remember when he died but it must have been while I was in the army or in the University at Austin, Texas.

Theron Bliss- Mr. Theron Bliss was another high school instructor that was the first Jewish person with whom I had any long term dealings. He, too, was in the Electrical Department at Tech and gave us the encouragement to fight the burden of minority prejudice. He could identify with the problem and recognized the "hunkey status" first generation Americans had at that time in that city.

He was always very supportive of us in our efforts to glean all we could from the program at Tech and worked hard at recommending work places to go to as well as those to avoid.

Helen W. Sampson- Helen W. Sampson was my Plane and Solid Geometry teacher in high school. Miss Sampson was one of the best and most sincere teachers that I have ever encountered in any teaching institution. Because of her rather large size she reminded me very much of Kate Smith who was my favorite female singer. Ms. Simpson demanded that each student work hard to keep up with the class assignments. She also had a unique ability to spot the students who needed special attention and then proceeded to give those students the opportunity to work out their lack of understanding - she usually solved the learning problem of the students sooner or later.

Joseph Jurlina

THE GENEALOGICAL ADVENTURE -- HOW IT ALL STARTED, WHERE IT WILL END

HOW IT ALL STARTED

It should be fairly evident after looking at my records that I am not and probably will never be a "real genealogist" having gotten involved only to gather what I could, about both Billie's and my families, in the relatively short time available to me.

Billie's cousin, Maxine Grable Cherryhomes, of Jacksboro, Jack County, Texas had secured the services of "professionals" to research the GRABLE side of her family. She was generous enough to share that information with us in great detail. As a result we knew much more about the GRABLES, Billie's father's side of the family, than we did about the VICKS, Billie's mother's side of the family.

In September of 1984 we received an invitation from Mrs. Mary Jo Brickell McCary, of Vicksburg, Mississippi to attend the dedication of a city park named for The Rev. Newitt H. Vick. The park is located on land which had been the Vick Plantation called "Open Woods" and actually included the graves of Newitt Vick and some members of his family. In addition to the dedication of the park, the 200th Anniversary of Methodism in Mississippi and the 170th Anniversary of the Crawford Street Methodist Church were to be commemorated. Mrs. McCary had found our names among in the Visitors roster of the Vicksburg Courthouse Museum. When we visited the Museum years before we had indicated that Billie was a Vick descendant searching for her ancestors in the library of the Museum since Vicksburg was named for Newitt Vick who had donated land to the City and to the Crawford Street Church.

Billie and I made photographs and slides of the ceremonies as well as an excellent video of the dedication and speeches. However, the video tape record was lost by being recorded over. I had planned to edit the video tape and forgot to remove the tape from the VCR and, as you might guess, I recorded something over the dedication ceremonies. This was one of the most traumatic experiences I have had in my adult life.

CITY BOY

Shortly after this occasion we learned that VICK family reunions had been held in Vicksburg for several years and the next one was scheduled for 7-9 June 1985 in Vicksburg so we made plans to attend. We attended the 1985 Reunion along with Barney and Kathryn Howell, Billie's cousin and her husband. We found so many nice folks involved in the search for their VICK roots and quite a bit of information already uncovered about the VICKS in America that we have tried to stay involved ever since. In fact, we have attended all reunions since 1985 except those in 1986 and 1997.

During the 1990 Reunion THE JOSEPH VICK FAMILY OF AMERICA, INC. was adopted as a name and incorporation papers as a non-profit corporation were subsequently filed in the State of North Carolina by O. Richard Wright. Richard is a Vick descendant and an attorney in Tabor City, North Carolina. Billie was elected as one of the eight members of the initial Board of Directors and served as Secretary from 1993 through 1999. I served as Treasurer for almost that same length of time and continued serving until about 2007 trying to get people interested in having another reunion but to no avail. Finally we got John Edward Vick to serve on the JVFOA Board. With his interest and energy another reunion was finally organized in 2008 as part of a Salado Vick family reunion. John and his wife Alta attended along with a few others of the JVFOA. By 2009, John was elected President of JVFOA and another reunion was held in Vicksburg, Mississippi which Billie and I could not attend. This seemed to stir the interest of some of the new members and a July, 2010 reunion was scheduled for Salt Lake City, Utah. Ed died of cancer in June of 2011.

WHERE WILL IT END

For most of the time since our first VICK Reunion I have not done too much information gathering about the JURLINA family; however, in September 1989 I purchased my first personal computer and shortly thereafter acquired the Morman Church LDS Genealogy program called Personal Ancestral File – PAF. After entering Billie's family data and what little I had on the JURLINA clan I decided to gather what I could before my time ran out and there was no one in my family to do some of the digging necessary for information.

Joseph Jurlina

Unknown to me, my cousin William George Avenmarg, oldest child of my Aunt Anna Telban Avenmarg, was researching his family roots. When we discovered our mutual interest in family history we began to exchange information. He has done a significant amount of research and documented his family data very well. I have entered all of his family data into my PAF database as well as the KRUMM family data provided to me by Mr. Lawrence Henry Krumm, our daughter's father-in-law. I addition, Billie's cousin Kathryn Brown Howell and her husband Barney Howell have given us much data for his HOWELL side of then family. To date, 15 April 2010, we have entered data for a little over 19,000 individuals into our PAF database.

During the fall of 1990 and early in 1991 I established contact with the family of Joseph John Jurlina in Columbus, Ohio and almost at the same time I wrote to some Jurlina kin in Jugoslavia at some addresses that were at least twenty five years old. Almost immediately I established that my long-held opinion that my name and age was very unique in the USA was incorrect. Mr. Joseph John Jurlina, from Columbus, Ohio, was born in Seline, Croatia, as was my father. Not only that but he had two sons, both born in Columbus - the oldest was named John Jurlina, with no middle name born on 22 February 1924, and the youngest was named Joseph Jurlina, with no middle name and born on 26 November 1925. Therefore, my long-held opinion about being a uniquely named individual was false.

Needless to say it has been an exciting time trying to put all the JURLINAS together into some sort of family. I have not been able to this date find any ties between the JURLINAS in Columbus and those in Cleveland. John Jurlina, from Columbus, had started doing family research after his retirement from NASA in Florida. We had established a great rapport but unknown to me he had a serious kidney ailment and he died on 30 March 1991 while in Virginia looking for a doctor who might arrange for a kidney transplant.

Since John's passing I have tried to contact cousins in foreign lands for information which might tie together all our loose ends. Sime Jurlina in Tivat/Brac, Croatia and Tome Jurlina in Belgrade, Serbia will probably be the best and most reliable sources. I recently found a family of Jurlinas in New Zealand which we will pursue in time.

CITY BOY

Sime Jurlina living in Tivat, Montenegro must have heard from one of our cousins since he sent us his family information out of the blue. Sime was born in 1939 in Slavonia and he married Nevenka Franceskovich about 1963. They have a son, Paul, born in 1965. Paul in turn married Tamara Gobovich in 1990 and they have a son, Antonio, born 26 May 1991. About 6-7 years ago we received a note from Sime saying that he and his wife Nevenka had moved to the Isle of Brac quite suddenly taking only that which they could carry in suitcases. Apparently Paul and his family stayed in Tivat where he is a practicing pharmacist. The only communication we have had from Sime recently was a photo of him and his wife. Sime's line goes back through Ante, son of Sime "Cipko". For now we have not identified the father of Cipko.

Unless I have told this before in this epistle, sometime in 1990 I decided to write to Ante Jurlina, son of my Uncle Sam who is my father's brother. I used an old address we had found in my Dad's belongings for Tome Jurlina in a suburb of Belgrade, Serbia. Within a few months I received a response from Tome and ever since we have established a series of communications - his in Serbo-Croatian and mine in English. This has required that he uses a daughter to translate my letters while I have had to resort to using whatever source was available each time he wrote. Generally I have resorted to asking Branka Petrovich of Sherman, Texas. Branka was born in Belgrade and does well in reading back contents of letters from Tome. On one or two occasions I have used Mr. Zivko "Geno" Ristevski, a soccer couch from Plano who married a Richardson teacher named Harriet.

Tome and I exchanged data for several years and in 1995 I prepared a three-ring notebook of data which summarized what he and I had developed to that point. As I recall the postage to get the report to Tome was about 60-70 dollars. It was shortly after I mailed that report to Tome that he wrote to me asking just what my intentions were with respect to that report. I told him all I was trying to do was to leave as much information about the Jurlina Clan in the USA and in Croatia as I could find in my remaining years. Billie and I sent him some money to enable him to make trips to Zadar from Belgrade to search the church files there.

Joseph Jurlina

In June of 2007 we received a report which Tome had written in Serbo-Croatian detailing all he had found about the Jurlinas in Croatia going back to our great-great-great grandfather Grgo Jurlina who was born about 1729. He also found that there were three different groups of Jurlinas who settled in areas near Seline - these included the Kudrovici, Cilovici and the Dolinari, the descendants of the three sons of Mate Jurlina. The three sons were Simon, Grgo and Tome. Our kin descended from Grgo through Nikola and Jacob. Ours were the Kudrovicic through Jacob born about 1755. If and when we get the report translated we will update this portion of the report.

RETIREMENT TRAVELS

TRIP TO CROATIA SUMMER 2004

Initially, our intent was to visit the Archives at Zagreb, Croatia and the Archives at Ljubljana, Slovenia to search for information about our Jurlina, Telban and Novak relatives, to visit the birthplaces of these relatives, and visit the retirement home in Seline of our cousin, Milan and Mira Jurlina, who have lived in Vancouver, BC, Canada for about 26 years. Milan, a machinist for Air Canada, was born in Seline and he plans to move to Seline after he retires. He and his wife and four boys have spent summer vacations in Seline for the last 20-years. They have constructed a three-story home on the same property his father and three brothers have constructed their homes. Milan and Mira's home faces in a NNW direction and is located less than 200 feet from the shore of an inlet of the Adriatic Sea. They "let" rooms to travelers in the summer. As it turned out our original plan was too ambitious for the time available. We did visit the Archives at Zagreb and were able to find some information not previously available to us. (The daily diary of our trip is in the appendix.)

AFTER OUR TRIP TO CROATIA IN 2001

Sometime after returning from Croatia I received a call from Anthony Buchic of Valpariso, Indiana. He related how he had just returned home from a trip to Croatia so talked a bit and began to realize we had crossed paths at the Zagreb airport as we were arriving there. He is working on his Bucich family story and discovered how many marriages occurred between our families over the years and offered to share some of his data.

I cannot now (October 2008) recall when he sent me a copy of birth records of Jurlinas which he had gleaned from records in Zadar. He probably made another trip in 2003 and sent the records in 2003 or 2004 as he had promised. He usually plans on a trip to Croatia every 2-3 years.

We continued to look for other sources of information about the Jurlina family and it was on such a hunt on the Internet that I found mention of the name of a Michael Jurlina in New Zealand who had been named Realtor of the Month. This peaked my interest so I sent an e-mail message to Michael telling him about us and our activities researching the Jurlinas from Croatia. I received an almost immediate response from Lisa Jurlina, Mike's wife, who obviously monitored their e-mail pretty closely. We exchanged e-mails in which I talked about the hope of visiting in their country of New Zealand.

In doing some further reading about New Zealand we discovered the "Dallies" of that country being a rather large group of Croatians from the south coast of Croatia in the region called Dalmatia who were involved in "gum digging" mostly on the North Island. The more we talked about New Zealand the more interest seemed to be generated among our family especially by Mike and Pamela. To get to the point more quickly, Pam and Mike thought visiting NZ was a great idea and convinced us that we should visit the NZ "Dallies" in July 2004. Pam and Mike made the plans for a trip from the 7th of July 2004 through the 19th of July. Without wasting any more time I communicated with Lisa & Mike Jurlina of NZ announcing our plan to be there about Sunday the 11th of July.

NEW ZEALAND 2004

To summarize the trip to and from New Zealand I would have to say we had a great and exciting time meeting the members of another limb of the Jurlina tree in New Zealand. We had the opportunity to meet 35 members of the Jurlina family there. We were also able to see the landscape, learn some history of New Zealand, take in a Rugby game, and were entertained royally. I suspect that Jacob had the best and most memorable time because he celebrated his 17th birthday with Ivan Jurlina and his family while there. (The full diary of the trip is in the appendix.)

WESTERN CARIBBEAN CRUISE 2010

Our children and grandchildren decided to organize a sea cruise in the Caribbean to celebrate our 85th birthdays and our anticipated 65th wedding anniversary of 12 May of 2010. You cannot imagine what a wonderful idea this was and Billie and I agreed with the concept whole heartedly and enjoyed it beyond our ability to describe.

We sailed out of Galveston, Texas harbor aboard the Royal Carribean ship named "VOYAGER OF THE SEAS" on 10 January 2010 for a seven day sea voyage with all 15 members of the Texas Jurlina clan aboard which included:

- Joseph Jurlina with wife Billie Grable Jurlina
- Carol Ann Jurlina Krumm and husband William Evans Krumm
- Michael Kenneth Jurlina and wife Pamela Hasty Jurlina
- Jacob and Sabrina Jurlina children of Michael and Pamela
- Jason Krumm, son of William and Carol Krumm
- Katherine Krumm Clark and Husband Ryan Michael Clark
- The Clark Children- Hope, Anastasia, Josiah, and Joshua

Our trip to Galveston by car was uneventful and we arrived in Galveston about 10 minutes before boarding on the Voyager of the Seas started. It was during this time that we were cautioned to have our passports ready for review by the crew. Billie had been carrying our passports in her purse so I did not worry about seeing them at that time. Unknown to me Billie had transferred them to her blue make-up bag. As we were moving along the line to the check-point someone suggested to Billie that she need not carry all the packages and bags she was carrying, so when the cart with all our bags came by en route to the ship Billie placed her make-up bag on the cart. Her first reaction was to check the make-up bag for something she thought should not be released but she could not immediately recall what it was so she replaced the make-up bag on the cart going to the ship baggage storage. By the time we reached the check point she remembered that the passports were already on their way to the baggage hold. We told the crew member what had happened but he insisted he had to see our passports. After much discussion and delay Michael, our son, decided he would try to find the bag and started out in a run toward the ship.

Time passed rather quickly and when there was only about two minutes left before the ship was to sail we had a message from the crew that Michael had found the bag. He had indeed found it after going through roughly a pile of five or six thousand bags already on the ship. With that we checked with the crew and started to board the ship as the tie lines were being freed from the ship. Michael was so out of breath that we had some serious concern about his condition but he assured us he was OK.

Billie also was so much relieved that she was in tears about the situation (and she wasn't the only one!).

As we set sail Billie and I were taken to our stateroom where we met a young girl from Norway who was to service our room. She had decorated our room to look like that of a young couple celebrating an anniversary and a sign on the door announcing our 65th anniversary of marriage. Needless to say we were as excited as could be with this sendoff. Our first meal at sea was wonderful as were all the meals afterward. We managed to eat with all the members of our family at breakfast and dinner.

After two days of sailing on a surprisingly smooth sea we arrived at Roatan Island off the coast of Honduras where we left the ship to visit the local port souvenir shops for about a two-hour stay. The shops were very interesting and had all sorts of souvenirs available as one would expect. The local natives were all eager to sell us whatever they had available representing their local culture. It was here that the Clark family took an excursion to the Gumbalimba Preservation Park where they were taken on a guided tour of the park. Apparently this was a most exciting tour since they were allowed to touch the animals and let the animals sit on their shoulders and hands. After the Clarks returned the party took a "ten minute" taxi ride to GIO's Seafood Restaurant on the other side of the peninsula. The children enjoyed looking at the fish and crabs off the restaurant dock. After lunch we returned to the ship to make picture of the port from the shipside. At dinner that night the ships' Chef Andrew came to see the Clark children and give them all chef hats as souvenirs. The children had met Chef Andrew earlier in the sailing to tell him about their intolerance to wheat and wheat products and to secure special menus for them.

The next day we arrived at Costa, Maya, Mexico to see what special things there were available to see and enjoy. Billie and I stayed aboard and enjoyed some of the views from the ship. After the others returned we all gathered at the miniature golf course on the top floor of the ship. Everyone in the party played and it was on one of the last holes that great granddad Jurlina "aced" the hole which drew quite a roar from the onlookers. Michael and Jacob were able to complete their certification as scuba divers while in port and were given the opportunity to do some scuba diving. Meanwhile the Clarks took a ride on a small submarine with glass walls below the water level so that they could make pictures of the marine life alongside the boat. There were 3-4 cruise ships moored in this port also.

The next day we were in Cozumel, Mexico. We went ashore and looked at the shops. Billie bought Sabrina a cute hair clip while Carol Ann bought a Mexican dress for her granddaughters. We stopped long enough to have a coke and ice cream bars in a small snack shop before returning to our ship.

After we set sail again that evening and just before dinner, the party gathered to have pictures made in various places. This included the one of the entire family party made by a fellow passenger who saw our need for a photographer. It was after dinner that great granddad found his way back to the Casino where he had spent some time trying to beat the slot machines. He admitted that at times he had won some large pots; however, he also admitted he ended up a small loser, ha!

Each night after dinner we were entertained with shows in the theater. On Saturday afternoon we went to an ice skating show.

The last night at sea on our return to Galveston turned out to be a rainy Saturday with the children at a special Adventure Ocean program while the adults played various games with dominoes. All in all the trip was an adventure that all involved will recall in days to come as "THAT GREAT SEA TRIP WE TOOK WITH ALL THE FAMILY PRESENT'!

Joseph Jurlina

SECOND FAMILY CARIBBEAN CRUISE

As John 1:16 says, "From the fullness of his grace we have all received one blessing after another." After that immense blessing, we were able to take another cruise together two years later, all except for our grandson, Jacob, who was busy at work in a relatively new position and thereby unable to receive the time off. This was a very similar cruise, also to the Western Caribbean with ports of call in Grand Cayman, Cozumel, and Costa Playa, Mexico. Taking our meals together, playing mini-golf, and drinking coffee after the shows for a full week was a joy for us all. Because Jason has been living in Haiti, Ryan, Katherine, and children live in New York, Sabrina is busy with college coursework, and Jacob has moved down to Houston to work, the opportunities we had on these two cruises to be together for a solid week, visiting and dining together was an enormous blessing to each of us.

CITY BOY

HIGHLAND SPRINGS

In December of 2010 we sold our home at 1244 Seminole Drive in Richardson and moved to a retirement complex just a few miles north in Dallas called Highland Springs. Here we have a bright, two-bedroom apartment custom decorated to match our furniture and possessions. We have really enjoyed making new friends and the opportunity to enjoy a renewed social life in these later retirement years. I am able to stop and work a puzzle for a while after meals. We regularly attend movie night with other couples. Billie has finally retired her gifts of cooking and hospitality and now enjoys the culinary work of others. Her orchids enjoy the greenhouse downstairs outside our apartment. The access to our physicians, only an elevator ride away (as is the post office!), along with so many other amenities has made Highland Springs the perfect next step for us. If you are ever in the Dallas area and are able, please come enjoy a meal with us.

Joseph Jurlina

APPENDIX A: PHOTOGRAPHS

TELBAN FAMILY

Mary Novak/Telban/Jeric/Virant
BORN 25 JANUARY 1882 -- DIED 28 OCTOBER 1948

Joseph Jurlina

JOSEPH JURLINA WITH MOTHER MARY TELBAN JURLINA 1927

CITY BOY

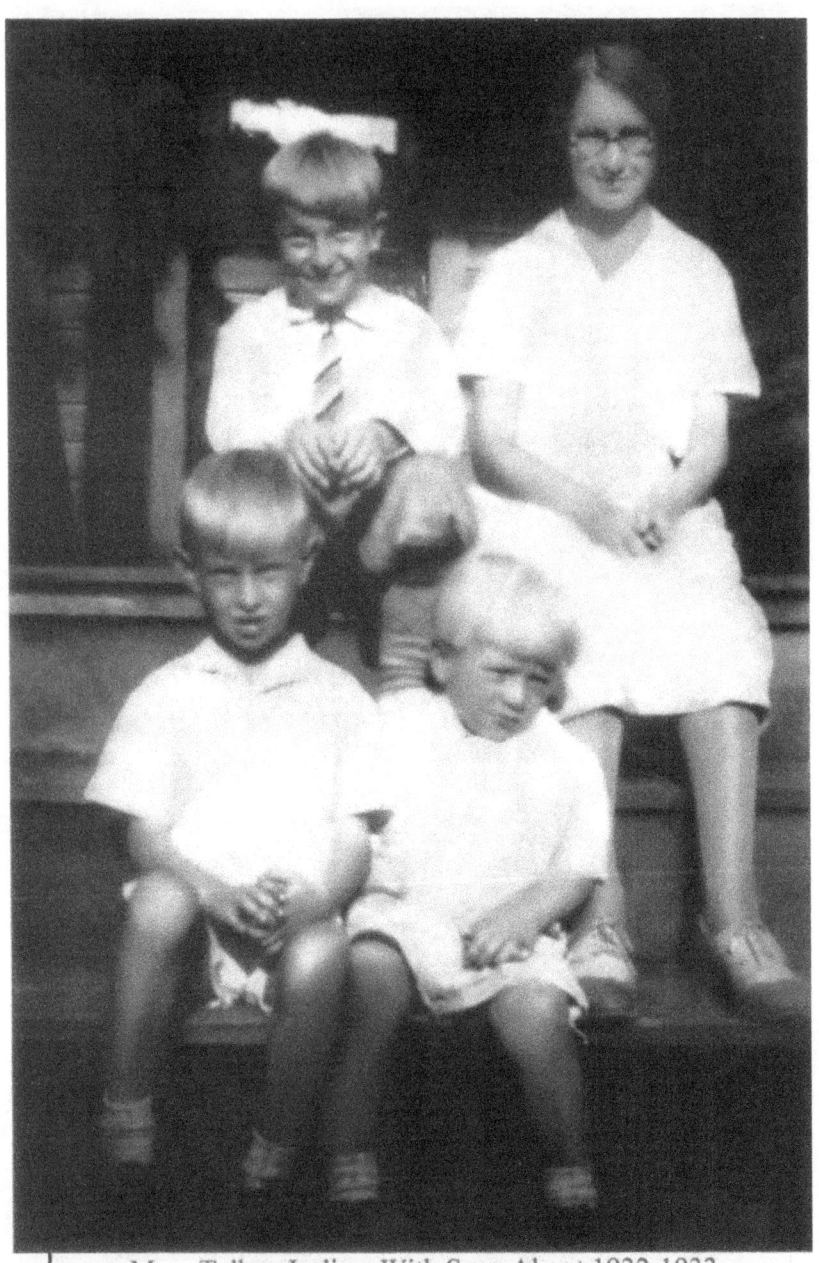

Mary Telban Jurlina, With Sons About 1932-1933
Joseph, oldest at abt. Nine Years, Thomas J. at abt. Six Years
Robert S. at abt. Four Years

Joseph Jurlina

GRANDMOTHER MARY TELBAN JURLINA WITH CAROL ANN
SUMMER 1947 IN AUSTIN, TX

CITY BOY

MARY TELBAN JURLINA – ABOUT 1942

Joseph Jurlina

MARY TELBAN JURLINA & ANNA TELBAN AVENMARG JASKO – ABT 1940

MARY JANE, MICHAEL, GRANDMOTHER MARY AND CAROL ANN – SUMMER 1953

CITY BOY

JOSEPHINE TELBAN ZERULL & HUSBAND FREDERICK ABT 1942

Joseph Jurlina

GRAMA TELBAN, BILL AVENMARG, ANNA TELAN AVENMARG & FRED AVENMARG, BILL'S FATHER – ABOUT 1944

CITY BOY

FRANCES TELBAN SIMONCIC WITH
JOAN. FRITZ (FRED/FREDERICK). MARGARET & JOSEPHINE TELBAN ZERULL ABT 1946

Joseph Jurlina

FRANCES, GENEVIEVE & JOSEPH SIMONCIC – ABOUT 1943

CITY BOY

TELBAN DESCENDANTS ABT. 1959

JULIA JERIC LASCO, DAVID & FATHER CHARLES "SKEEZIX" LASCO – ABOUT 1960

AUNT ANGELA TELBAN PASTWA & LINDA JURLINA ABOUT 1960
AT LINDA'S PARENTS HOME ON 74TH STREET

CITY BOY

GENEVIEVE SIMONCIC WITH HUSBAND RICHARD LASKOWSKI WITH CHILDREN LAURA, RICHARD & LYNN ABT 1961

Joseph Jurlina

CITY BOY

WILLIAM GEORGE & BONNIE IRENE MCLAIN AVENMARG – 1988
1926 – 2001   1923-2005

Joseph Jurlina

BLAKE & JONI AVENMARG – 23 JUNE 2002

CITY BOY

THOMAS JURLINA

Joseph Jurlina

THOMAS JURLINA & NEWST AT POP'S WORKPLACE – APRIL 1933

THOMAS JURLINA WITH DAUGHTER MARY JANE ABT 1942

Joseph Jurlina

THOMAS JOHN JURLINA WITH FATHER THOMAS – APRIL 1943 AT 1157 E. 63 ST. CLEVELAND, OHIO

CITY BOY

Joseph Jurlina

THOMAS JURLINA – DECEMBER 1962
AT T.J. & LEONA'S NEW HOME

CITY BOY

JURLINA RELATIVES

JOSEPH JURLINA, BORN 2 JANUARY 1859, DIED 26 JULY 1939

FATHER OF THOMAS JURLINA, BORN 31 MAY 1896, DIED 22 OCTOBER 1979

GRANDFATHER OF JOSEPH, EDWARD, THOMAS J., ROBERT S. & MARY JANE

Joseph Jurlina

JOSEPH JURLINA IN SELINE, CROATIA – ABT 1938
FATHER OF THOMAS JURLINA

2 JANUARY 1859   26 JULY 1939

CITY BOY

Sima Jurkiwa
Born Feb 1st, 1900

To my dear brother
to remember our family home

Joseph Jurlina

SAM JURLINA, BORN 1 FEB. 1900, SON OF JOSEPH, BROTHER OF THOMAS, FATHER OF TOME WHO WAS BORN IN 1928

TOME JURLINA, BORN 27 APRIL 1928 SON OF SAM, HUSBAND OF BEBA & SOURCE OF MUCH FAMILY DATA

CITY BOY

CHILDREN OF THOMAS AND MARY JURLIN, SIBLINGS OF JOSEPH

ROBERT STEPHEN JURLINA – ABT 1932

Joseph Jurlina

ROBERT S. JURLINA WITH SISTER MARY JANE
1941

CITY BOY

THOMAS JOHN "TJ" JURLINA H.S. GRADUATION JUNE 1945

ROBERT STEPHEN JURLINA H.S. GRADUATION – JUNE 1947

LEONA MALNAR AND THOMAS "TJ" JURLINA EASTER 1948

Joseph Jurlina

SISTER MARY JANE JURLINA EASTER 1948

THOMAS "TJ" JURLINA & MRS. LEONA JURLINA
22 JULY 1950

Joseph Jurlina

MARY JANE JURLINA H.S. GRADUATION - JUNE 1959

CITY BOY

ROBERT, MARY JANE & THOMAS JURLINA – 1959

Joseph Jurlina

LINDA JURLINA BAZNIK & HER FATHER "TJ" JURLINA – 1963 ?

LEONA & THOMAS J. JURLINA WITH CHIDREN THOMAS A., LINDA & NANCY - 1966

Joseph Jurlina

ROBERT JURLINA/ DOROTHY THALER WEDDING 15 NOV., 1969

NANCY JURLINA/GREG PROSSER WEDDING ON 17 JULY 1981

Joseph Jurlina

Greg & Nancy (Jurlina) Prosser, Ryan, Anna, & Alan

CITY BOY

228

Joseph Jurlina

Nancy Prosser, Linda Baznik, Leona Jurlina, and Tom Jurlina

CITY BOY

Grown children and spouses of brother, Thomas

Greg Prosser, Mary & Tom, Nancy Prosser, Linda & Ed Baznik

Joseph Jurlina

Linda & Ed Baznik **with children Michael, Stephen, Emily & Ed**

CITY BOY

Emily, Ed, Stephen, & Michael

Joseph Jurlina

Mary, Peter, Merielle, & Tom Jurlina

CITY BOY

BOB JURLINA WITH POP'S WINE PRESS REMNANTS

Brother, Bob and Ella Jurlina with Billie and Joe

CITY BOY

JOE'S SISTER MARY JANE & HUSBAND BILL ELAM – 22 JUNE 2002

Joseph Jurlina

Mary Jane & Bill Elam, Kristy, Michael, & Jennifer

Gabriella, Michael, Tina & Owen Elam - 2006

Kristy with husband, Brian Hulsey

CITY BOY

Joseph Jurlina

Counsins meet for lunch once a year

Joe with sister Mary Jane, cousins Genevieve Ward and Elsie Yeck, and brother Bob the night before the anniversary party

Together at Joe & Billie's 60th wedding anniversary party

CITY BOY

BILLIE GRABLE'S ENGAGEMENT PICTURE – 13 APRIL 1945

**Barney Lee Howell & F. Kathryn Brown Marriage on 23 November 1946
In Throckmorton, Texas with Mother Alpha Lee Murray Brown in background**

BILLIE & JOE ON THE BANK OF THE NIAGRA RIVER JUST BELOW THE FALLS – 1952

Joseph Jurlina

CAROL ANN, JOE, BILLIE & MICHAEL ABOUT FEB., 1955

CAROL ANN, MICHAEL, BILLIE AND JOSEPH – SPRING OF 1965 IN 20TH YEAR OF MARRIAGE

Joseph Jurlina

40TH ANNIVERSARY CAKE ON 12 MAY 1985

Joseph Jurlina

APRIL 2000 AUSTIN, TX
50TH ANNIVERSARY REUNION
ON CAMPUS OF
THE UNIVERSITY OF TEXAS
AT AUSTIN, TEXAS

Joseph Jurlina

TEXAS JURLINA CLAN AT 60TH WEDDING ANNIVERSARY CELEBRATED ON 29 MAY 2005 IN DALLAS, TX
WEDDING TOOK PLACE ON 12 MAY 1945 IN WICHITA FALLS, TX

THE CLARK, KRUMM & JURLINA FAMILIES AT THE LAKE HOUSE OF MICHAEL & PAMELA JURLINA AT CEDAR CREEK LAKE ON 25 MAY 2008

Joseph Jurlina

CLOSE FRIENDS OVER THE YEARS

REN & EDWARD VEIGEL WITH DAUGHTER SANDY IN 1947

MIKE, MATILU AND TED HATCHER – NOVEMBER 1952

SYLVIA AND LEE WITH CHILDREN DAVID, TIM & BECKY – SPRING 1953

JOANNE & WILL BELL RETURNING FROM ENGLAND – JUNE 1980

Joseph Jurlina

JAMES T. & GLENNIE BYRON RETURN FROM ENGLAND – JUNE 1980

CITY BOY

BARNEY & KATHRYN HOWELL, BILLIE & JOE, LEE & SYLVIA GRIFFIN – MAY 1995

Margene and Jerry Parr- teacher friend of Billie's

Lemuel and Beth LaRue, friends from UT

CITY BOY

APPENDIX B: DOCUMENTS

Joseph Jurlina

SUPPLEMENTAL REPORT OF BIRTH
STATE OF OHIO

(This return should be made by the local Registrar)

Reg. Dist. No.
Primary Dist. No.
Place of birth .... No. 87 .... St. .... Registry Number ....

I HEREBY CERTIFY that the child described herein has been named Mary Telban

(Give name, in full)
(Signature) Mary Telban
(Address) ....
(Local Registrar)

SEX OF CHILD: F
Number in order of birth: 1
DATE OF BIRTH: June 2, 1903
FATHER: John Telban
MOTHER (Maiden Name): Mary Novak

RETURN OF A BIRTH

To the Secretary of the Public Health Division:
102 CITY HALL,
THE CITY OF CLEVELAND, O.
DEPARTMENT OF POLICE.

I hereby report the following Report of a Birth:

Date of Birth 2 day of June 1904 Sex Female Color White
Place of Birth 252 Bayior St. Street.
Name of child (if any has been given) Martha
Maiden name of Mother Mary Novak
Name of Mother at date of birth of child Mary Telban
Nativity of Mother Austrian Age 22 Color White
Full name of Father John Telban (Telgan)
Nativity of Father Austrian Age 27 Color White
Name of Medical attendant, or Midwife Wilhelmia Merrett
Residence of same 252 William Ave.

APPLICATION No.		FILED AND MARRIAGE LICENSE ISSUED		1922
Name	Thomas Yurlina	Name	Mary Telban	
Age 26 Residence	1312 E. 55th St.	Age 18 Residence	798 E. 156th St.	
Place of Birth	Austria	Place of Birth	Cleveland, O	
Occupation	Laborer	Occupation	None	
Father's Name	Joseph	Father's Name	John	
Mother's Maiden Name	Mary Marinkovic	Mother's Maiden Name	Mary Novak	
Number of times previously married	None	Number of times previously married	None	
		Married Name		

Marriage to be solemnized by Rev. J. Skur, Holmes Ave. License issued by Frank Zizelman Deputy Clerk
Consent of: .... Filed .... 19 .... Consent of .... Filed .... 19 ....

THE STATE OF OHIO, } ss.
CUYAHOGA COUNTY,

RETURN

I CERTIFY, That on the 11th day of November 1922, Mr. Thomas Yurlina and Miss Mary Telban were by me legally joined in marriage.

Rev. Joseph Skur

CITY BOY

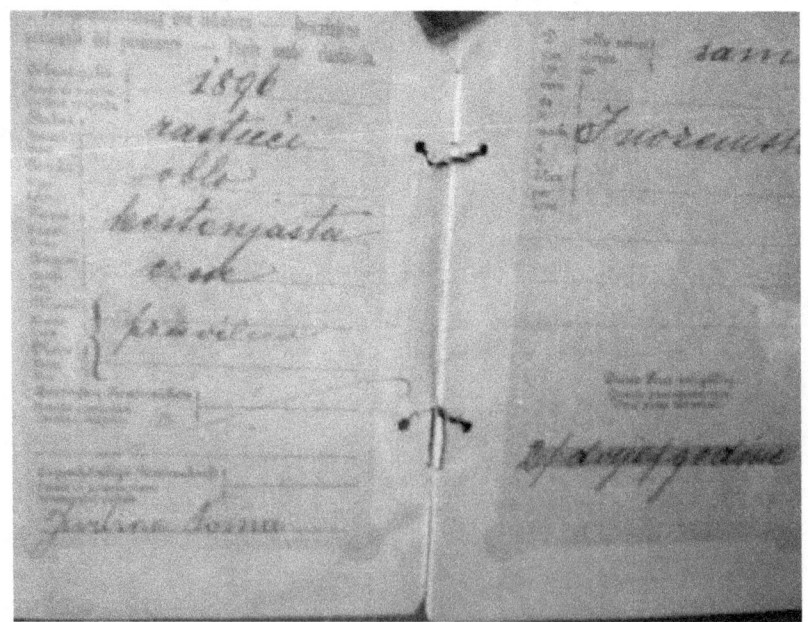

Joseph Jurlina

N° 83649 A

Copy of Birth Certificate
REGISTRATION DISTRICT No. 8118

FIFTY CENTS

DEPARTMENT OF PUBLIC WELFARE
DIVISION OF HEALTH
BUREAU OF VITAL STATISTICS
CITY OF CLEVELAND
STATE OF OHIO

Registered No. 16121

PLACE OF BIRTH County of Cuyahoga, City of Cleveland, No. 1157 E. 63rd Street
(If birth occurred in a hospital or institution, give its NAME instead of street and number)

FULL NAME OF CHILD ..... Joseph Jurlina

Sex of Child: Male | Twin, triplet or other? (To be answered only in event of plural births) | Number in order of birth | Legitimate? Yes | Date of birth: September 19th, 1924

FULL NAME Father: Thomas Jurlina
RESIDENCE Including P. O. Address: 1157 E. 63rd Street
AGE AT LAST BIRTHDAY: 27 (Years)
COLOR OR RACE: White
Birthplace (city or country): Jugo-Slavia
OCCUPATION:
a. Trade, profession, or particular kind of work done, as spinner, sawyer, bookkeeper, etc.: Laborer
b. Industry or business in which work was done, as silk mill, sawmill, bank, etc.
c. Date (month and year) last engaged in this work ..... 19....
e. Total time (years) spent in this work

Number of children of this mother (At time of this birth and including this child):
(a) born alive and now living: 1
(b) born alive but now dead:
If stillborn, period of gestation ..... months or weeks | Cause of stillbirth ......

FULL MAIDEN NAME Mother: Mary Telban
RESIDENCE Including P. O. Address: 1157 E. 63rd Street
AGE AT LAST BIRTHDAY: 20 (Years)
COLOR OR RACE: White
Birthplace (city or country): U.S.
OCCUPATION:
d. Trade, profession, or particular kind of work done, as housekeeper, typist, nurse, clerk, etc.: Housewife
e. Industry or business in which work was done, as own home, laundry office, silk mill, etc.
f. Date (month and year) last engaged in this work ..... 19....
h. Total time (years) spent in this work

Is child congenitally deformed? No
Was Prophylactic against Ophthalmia Neonatorum used? Yes

Before labor ....
During labor ....

CERTIFICATE OF ATTENDING PHYSICIAN OR MIDWIFE

I hereby certify that I attended the birth of this child, who was Alive (Born Alive or Stillborn) at 4.9 a. m. on the date above stated.

(Signed) Maryane Puc ..... Midwife M. D.
Address 1085 E. 64th Street

..... 23rd, 24, J.C. Smith, M.D.

Cleveland, Ohio, this ..... day of ..... MAY 20 1942

State of Ohio, County of Cuyahoga } I, ... of Registration District 8118, as provided by an act establishing a Bureau of Vital Statistics, and to provide for the prompt and permanent registration of all Births and Deaths occurring within the State of Ohio, do hereby certify that the within copy is taken and copied from the records of this office and that the same is a correct transcript thereof. In testimony whereof, I have hereunto subscribed my name at

Registrar

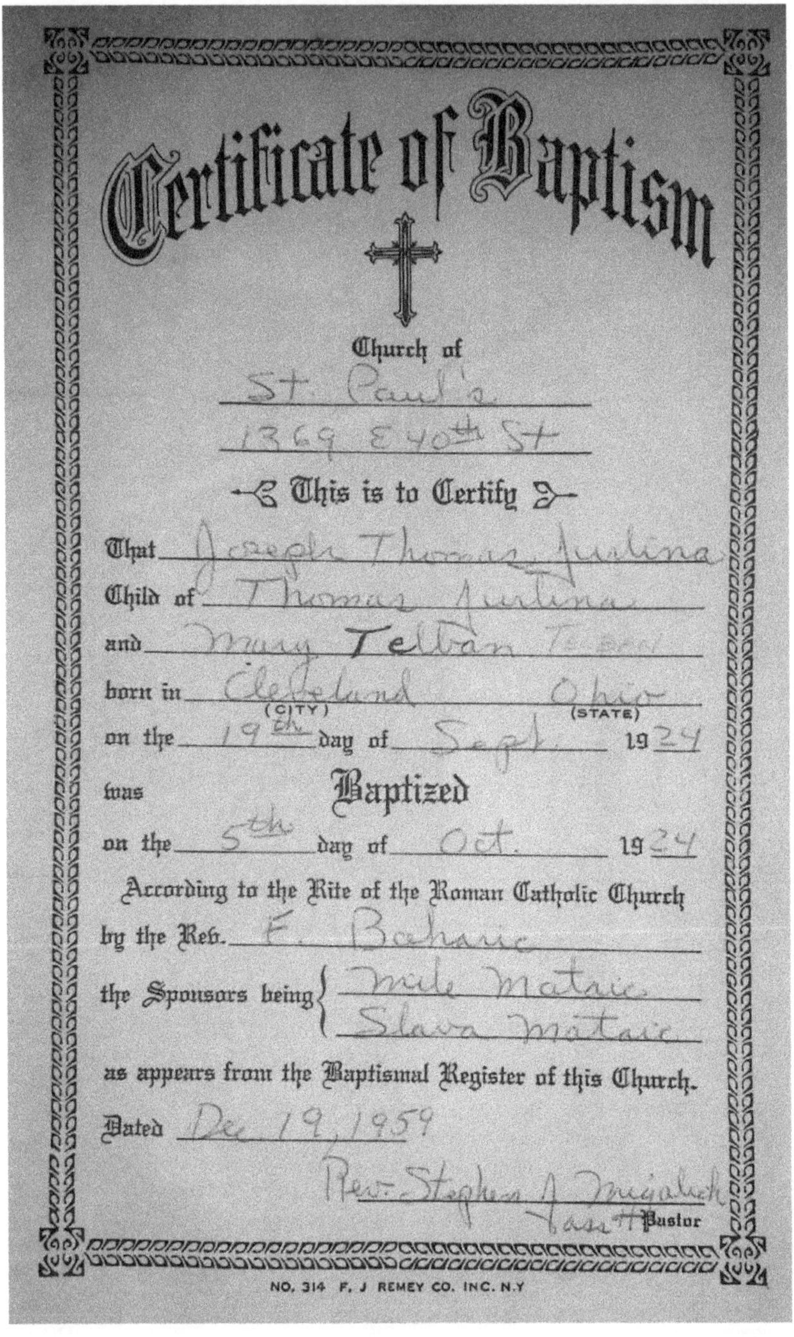

Certificate of Baptism

Church of St Paul's
1369 E 40th St

— This is to Certify —

That Joseph Thomas Jurlina
Child of Thomas Jurlina
and Mary Telban Telban
born in Cleveland, Ohio
on the 19th day of Sept. 1924
was Baptized
on the 5th day of Oct. 1924
According to the Rite of the Roman Catholic Church
by the Rev. F. Baharic
the Sponsors being { Mile Mataic
Slava Mataic

as appears from the Baptismal Register of this Church.

Dated Dec. 19, 1959

Rev. Stephen J. Migalich
Pastor

NO. 314 F. J. REMEY CO. INC. N.Y

Joseph Jurlina

from the desk of **Bill Avenmarg**

For Your Info:

Joseph Jurlina - Baptized 10-5-24
Godparents - Mile Mataic - Slava Mataic

Edward Jurlina - Baptized 7-4-26
Godparents - Pasko Stanic - Catherine Stanic

Thomas Jurlina - Baptized 1-8-28
Godparents - Joseph Dadic - Franica Telban

Robert Jurlina - Baptized 1-19-30
Godparents - John Benko - Dorothy Benko

Mary Jane Jurlina - Baptized 6-8-41
Godparents - Joseph Simoncic - Frances Simoncic

All But Mary Jane Baptized at
St Paul Church - 40th St -
Mary Jane Baptized at St. Vitus

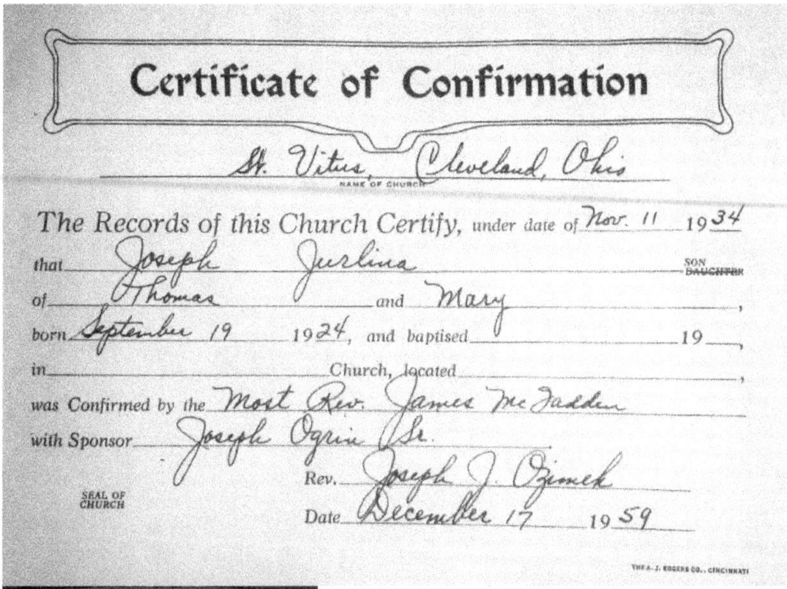

Joseph Jurlina

Certificate of Confirmation

St. Vitus, Cleveland, Ohio

The Records of this Church Certify, under date of Nov. 11 19 34 that Joseph Jurlina of Thomas and Mary, born September 19 19 24, and baptised _____ 19__ in _____ Church, located _____, was Confirmed by the Most Rev. James McFadden with Sponsor Joseph Ogrin Sr.

Rev. Joseph J. Ozimek
Date December 17 19 59

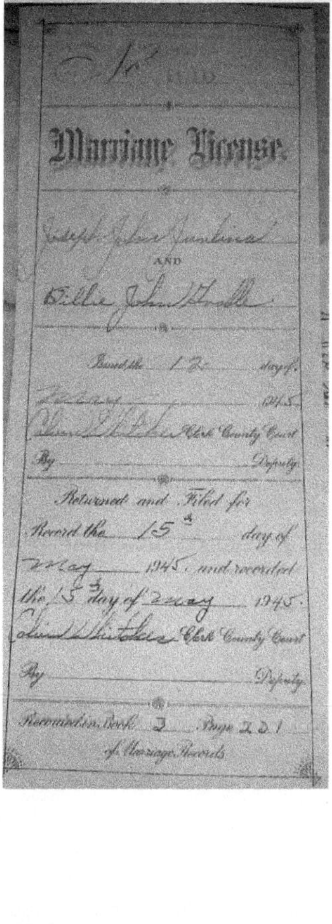

Marriage License

Joseph John Jurlina
AND
Billie John Thralls

Issued the 17 day of
February 1945.
_____ Clerk County Court
By _____ Deputy.

Returned and Filed for
Record the 15ᵈ day of
May 1945, and recorded
the 15ᵈ day of May 1945.
_____ Clerk County Court
By _____ Deputy.

Recordation Book 3 Page 221
of Marriage Records

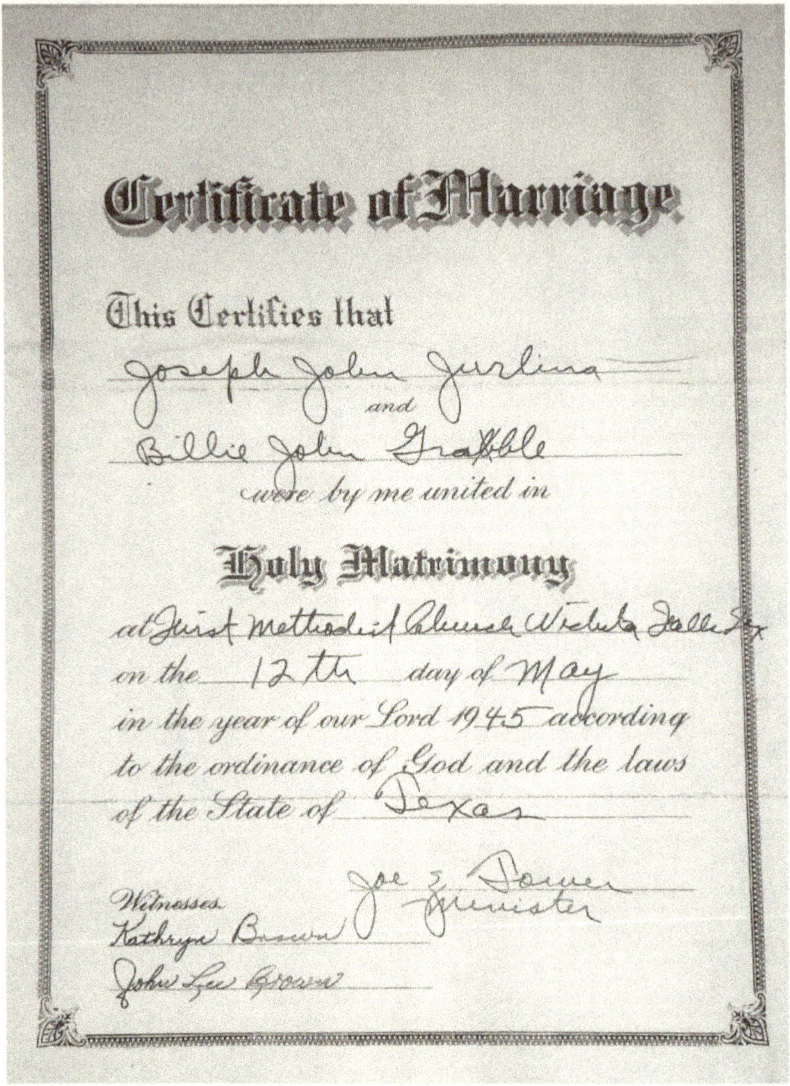

CITY BOY

Certificate of Marriage

This Certifies that

Joseph John Jurlina

and

Billie John Grabble

were by me united in

Holy Matrimony

at First Methodist Church Wichita Falls Tx on the 12th day of May in the year of our Lord 1945 according to the ordinance of God and the laws of the State of Texas

Witnesses   Joe E. Bowen
Kathryn Brown   Minister
John Lee Brown

Joseph Jurlina

App. not Req.

Prepare in Duplicate

Local Board No. 39
Cuyahoga County   035
FEB 23 1943   02a
4900 Euclid Ave.
Cleveland Ohio
(LOCAL BOARD DATE STAMP WITH CODE)

February 23, 1943
(Date of mailing)

ORDER TO REPORT FOR INDUCTION

The President of the United States,

To ____ Joseph ____ - ____ Jurlina ____
(First name)   (Middle name)   (Last name)

Order No. __11782__

GREETING:

Having submitted yourself to a local board composed of your neighbors for the purpose of determining your availability for training and service in the land or naval forces of the United States, you are hereby notified that you have now been selected for training and service therein.

You will, therefore, report to the local board named above at __Rm. 310, 4900 Euclid Bldg.__
(Place of reporting)

at __7:00 a.__ m., on the __10th__ day of __March__, 19 __43.__
(Hour of reporting)

This local board will furnish transportation to an Induction station. You will there be examined, and, if accepted for training and service, you will then be inducted into the land or naval forces.

Persons reporting to the induction station in some instances may be rejected for physical or other reasons. It is well to keep this in mind in arranging your affairs, to prevent any undue hardship if you are rejected at the induction station. If you are employed, you should advise your employer of this notice and of the possibility that you may not be accepted at the induction station. Your employer can then be prepared to replace you if you are accepted, or to continue your employment if you are rejected.

Willful failure to report promptly to this local board at the hour and on the day named in this notice is a violation of the Selective Training and Service Act of 1940, as amended, and subjects the violator to fine and imprisonment.

If you are so far removed from your own local board that reporting in compliance with this order will be a serious hardship and you desire to report to a local board in the area of which you are now located, go immediately to that local board and make written request for transfer of your delivery for induction, taking this order with you.

Member or clerk of the local board.

D. S. S. Form 150

Army of the United States

Honorable Discharge

This is to certify that

JOSEPH JURLINA

35052774 STAFF SERGEANT HEADQUARTERS BATTERY 664TH FIELD ARTILLERY BATTALION

Army of the United States

is hereby Honorably Discharged from the military service of the United States of America.

This certificate is awarded as a testimonial of Honest and Faithful Service to this country.

Given at SEPARATION CENTER
CAMP ATTERBURY INDIANA

Date 2 FEBRUARY 1946

Reid H. McLain

REID H. McLAIN
MAJOR, A. C.

Joseph Jurlina

Tužnim srcem svim javljamo rođacima prijateljima i znancima žalosnu vijest da nam je naš dragi i nezaboravni suprug, otac, brat, djed, šogor, svekar, tesak i stric, gospodin

Antun Jurlina

u nedjelju dne 15. XI u 10 sati u 71. godini života nakon duge i teške bolesti blago u Gospodinu preminuo

Pogreb dragog nam pokojnika obavit će se u četvrtak dne 19. XI u 15:30 sati iz mrtvačnice na Mirogoju.

Sv misa zadušnica služit će se u *petak* dne *20/XI* u *8* sati ujutro u župnoj crkvi Marije Pomoćnice,

U Zagrebu, 16. XI 1964.

POČIVAO U MIRU BOŽJEM

Vesna, Ivančica, Biserka, Jasminka i Ljerka - unuke
Anka i Nevenka - snahe
Šime, Tomo i Anka - braća
i ostala tugujuća rodbina
Antonija - supruga
Rudolf i Ivica - sinovi

With sad heart we like to inform our relatives and friends that our husband, father, brother, grandfath brothe in law, father in law and uncle

Antun Jurlina

past away on Sunday 15.XI at 10:00 after long illness was 71 years old and present himself befor the Lord.

Funeral of our lovedone will be on 19-XI, 15:30 from Funeral Home at Mirogoj cametary.

Mass will be Fri. 20.XI, 7:30 at St Mary's Church.

Zagrab, 16.XI.1964

Rest in peace with Lord.

Grandaughters: Vesna, Ivančica, Biserka, Jasminka and Ljerka
Daughters in Law: Anka and Nevenka.
Brothers: Šime, Tomo and Anka (sister)
Wife: Antonija. Sons: Rudolf and Ivica.

CITY BOY

AMERIŠKA DOMOVINA, MAY 29, 1987

by Vince Gostilna

On March 1st, Mr. Joseph Novak, well known former St. Clair businessman, celebrated his 90th birthday with his family at his Nottingham Road home.

The one-time owner of Novak's Confectionery and Card Shop at E. 62nd and St. Clair (see photos), Joe has been retired since 1972. He hasn't aged a bit, and is still active, keeping his comfortable home in trim shape. For exercise, he daily walks in the picturesque and verdant Nottingham Road vicinity. He is also often seen at St. Vitus on Sundays, attending Mass.

Mr. Novak was born in Smarjeta Toplice of Slovenia on March 1, 1897. He was the only son born to Joseph and Mary Novak. There were five sisters who, like their brother, immigrated to the United States. All except Joe have since died.

As a stripling lad of 15 Joe came to Cleveland in 1912 and secured gainful employment until 1920 when he opened his confectionery at 6128 St. Clair. Three years earlier, young Novak married the lovely Mary Milavec. The wedding ceremony was performed by then Rev. B. J. Ponikvar in the old wooden St. Vitus Church on Norwood.

In a short time Novak's business venture succeeded, having prized franchises with Hallmark cards, Schaffts candy and "Cleveland" ice cream. In addition, the store featured a tobacco section. In 1929 a refrigerated soda fountain was installed, the first such electrical unit in the area.

The soda bar became very popular with the many workers from nearby plants, coming at noon to sip on delicious and refreshing sodas, malts and other delights.

The years during the 20's and 30's went by quickly, especially since Joe and Mary Novak were kept busy by their many satisfied customers who made Novak's store their favorite stopping place.

Just when things seemed to be going even better for the popular couple, their luck was quickly transformed into misfortune. On that terrible day of Oct. 20, 1944 the East Ohio Gas Explosion rocked the entire area. Especially affected was the street in front of Novaks' which exploded, causing a parked fire engine to fall into the large crater.

The building which housed Novaks' Confectionery suffered serious structural damage that necessitated razing it.

The Novaks' initially intended to resume their immensely popular establishment in a new building, but things did not turn out as they had hoped. Instead, Joe and Mary Novak opened up a small card shop a few doors west in the Svete family properties. With their large selection of fine greeting cards and chocolates, they resumed their business on a somewhat more limited scale.

The Novak couple decided it was time to retire in 1972 after 52 years in business on St. Clair Ave.

Just five years after closing, Joe's wonderful wife, Mary, passed away on May 17, 1977. Since that time Joe Novak has been busy in maintaining his well-kept home along with his son, Ernie and daughter-in-law, Emma, enabling his two grandchildren to visit with him often and thus Joe Novak is spending his retirement years in a fine fashion.

Our wish is that Joe has many more healthy and happy years.

Joseph Jurlina

APPENDIX C: TRIP DIARIES

OUR TRIP TO SELINE, CROATIA 24 JUNE – 4 JULY 2001

SUMMARY OF TRIP

Michael Jurlina and his family and parents (Pamela, Jacob, Sabrina, Joseph and Billie) started this journey from the D/FW airport aboard an American Airlines Boeing 777 at 2:40 PM on Sunday, 24 June 2001. Flight 38 landed at Zurich, Switzerland at 10:30 AM on 25 June 2001. The Zurich airport was the first airport I had seen with a fresh-fruit market in the terminal. It had many lovely shops. We departed Zurich at about 12:20 PM on 25 June aboard Swiss Air Flight 1200 for about a one-hour flight to Zagreb, Croatia aboard a British made 4-engine jet plane, arriving in Zagreb about 1:20 PM. The Zagreb airport looked like a first-class shopping mall.

Initially, our intent was to visit the Archives at Zagreb, Croatia and the Archives at Ljubljana, Slovenia to search for information about our Jurlina, Telban and Novak relatives, to visit the birthplaces of these relatives, and visit the retirement home in Seline of our cousin, Milan and Mira Jurlina, who have lived in Vancouver, BC, Canada for about 26 years. Milan, a machinist for Air Canada, was born in Seline and he plans to move to Seline after he retires. He and his wife and four boys have spent summer vacations in Seline for the last 20-years. They have constructed a three-story home on the same property his father and three brothers have constructed their homes. Milan and Mira's home faces in a NNW direction and is located less than 200 feet from the shore of an inlet of the Adriatic Sea. They "let" rooms to travelers in the summer.

As it turned out our original plan was too ambitious for the time available. We did visit the Archives at Zagreb and were able to find some information not previously available to us - more about that later.

MONDAY, 25 JUNE 2001

CITY BOY

Three young men met us when we arrived in Zagreb about 1:20 PM. They were: Nikola "Nick" Jurlina, youngest son of Milan Jurlina, second cousin once removed, and two friends of Nick's named Nikola and Mate (Nick and Matthew). They were in a car owned and driven by Nickola the friend of our Nick and led us into the center of Zagreb and our Hotel Sheraton – a drive of about 20 minutes. We followed in our rented Ford "Transit" Van. The Van had a 4-cylinder diesel engine that responded very well after Mike became accustomed to driving the standard stick-shift transmission.

All of our "leaders" were enrolled in universities. Our Nick and Mate were students at Zagreb University while the second Nick was a senior at West Point in the USA. The West Point Cadet, was a senior and entered West Point as a member of the Croatian Army. West Point accepts one new student from the Croatian Army each year and Nick was a member of that Army – he will serve six-years in the Croatian Army after graduation. At the Sheraton we checked in and then six Americans and three Croatians stopped for drinks and conversation in the lobby.

We discovered that the two Nicks had grown up together and attended private Roman Catholic Schools in Vancouver, BC, Canada. Matthew was born in Croatia and had attended a University in London as a student of Forestry but in Zagreb has changed his major to English. Nick, the soldier, was a System Engineering Student, while "our" Nick is working toward a degree in Pharmacy rather than one in medicine as originally planned. His brother, Hrvoje (Hrv), who we met later in the day, is a senior medical student in Zagreb and planned to specialize in pediatrics after his internship. All the young men now plan to stay in Zagreb after their school and military commitments are fulfilled. Since our visit in 2001, Hrv has completed his medical studies, married and has one child. They live in Zagreb.

That afternoon, the boys returned to their dorms to study for final exams while the American Tourists took a stroll to view the neighborhood and find a place to eat dinner. The GUSTEK Restaurant, just a few blocks from the hotel, looked promising because the costs were reasonable and the ladies liked the menu and the ambiance. Robert, our waiter, was very friendly so we expected a pleasant meal; however, just as we finished ordering our meal the lights went out. After several minutes, Robert informed us that the cooks would not be able to cook our meals and in fact refused to stay in the dark. He let us know about the situation and gave us the option of staying for cheese and cold snacks or leaving. We chose to stick out the adventure and were served a variety of cheese, crackers and bread. It was a nice experience. Of course, just about the time we started to leave the lights came back on.

After our meal we walked up to and into the railroad station (Kolodvor) then walked down the divided roadway facing the station past the large public buildings on either side until we reached the street on which the hotel was located. It was a long day so we looked forward to a good nights rest.

TUESDAY, 26 JUNE 2001

Nick, Hrv and the American Tourists continued their walk around town taking pictures as we walked. In the large city square we came upon a puppeteer who had his puppet playing a small piano, with movable keys but no strings, keeping time with the music supplied by a "boombox". This was rather fascinating so we all stopped to watch the performance. We then walked through a large glass-domed building that turned out to be a shopping mall with many retail stores. The glass roof was very nice and unusual so we took pictures from under the dome. We continued our walk around the square in Old Zagreb as Hrv told us about the statue of King Tomislav mounted on his horse looking over New Zagreb. While Croatia was under the control of the Serbian Communists the statue was faced toward Serbia in the east; however, since the Republic of Croatia has severed its ties to Serbia the statue now faces New Zagreb to the south. We finally got a better view of the 10th Century Cathedral of St. Stephen's in Zagreb that was undergoing a massive removal and replacement of the outer stone face.

We walked up about 200 steps to the walled city where we came upon St. Mark's Church with its very colorful red and white tiled roof. The bell tower of this church is marked as having been erected in 1841; however, the church probably dates back to the ninth century or earlier.

CITY BOY

As we left St. Mark's we saw an old gate, very much like some we saw in Germany in 1976 - this one had a date of 760 inscribed over the entrance. A story is told about this gate in which a miracle happened during a conflict many years ago, details of which were not known by our group, and ever since local people stop to offer prayers at a shrine installed many years ago. We passed through the tunnel and stopped for refreshments at a "pub" which was located just across from a statue of St. George and the slain dragon.

We walked up Skalenska Street to Cathedral of St. Stephen's that dates back to the early days of Zagreb in which many works of early 16th Century German artist Albrecht Drurer are on display. This structure is undergoing a total reconstruction of the exterior stone facing – one stone at a time. The structure with a pointed silo-looking roof is one end of the Bishop's Rectory located on two sides of and behind the Cathedral. Note the original organ is still in use. On a marble wall over a side altar is a message inscribed in an ancient alphabet that predates the Cyrillic alphabet used in Russia and the eastern part of the former Jugoslavia – Hrv gave us a card with this alphabet and the modern Cyrillic side by side.

After the tour of the Cathedral we went across the Cathedral Square and ate dinner at a Croatian Restaurant Kapitolska Klet (sp). As we were leaving, a Japanese lady guest wanted to make a video of the Americans so we obliged her and then made a video of her. After dinner, we walked back to the Sheraton.

WEDNESDAY, 27 JUNE 2001

Wednesday morning Hrv and Nick came by the hotel to visit briefly before Nick and I returned to the Archives to review microfilm records. I showed the JURLINA FAMILY TREE printout to them and tried to impress them that there were many blanks yet to be filled out.

Jacob took the video camera and joined his parents and Grandmother on a visit around metropolitan Zagreb. Apparently, they had a great day visiting a castle, and on leaving, trying to explain to two police officers why they were going the wrong way on a one-way street. Michael treated the policemen to drinks at the castle as he had to turn the van around and return from whence he had come.

THURSDAY, 28 JUNE 2001

We drove to Novo Mesto and Ljubljana in Slovenia to look for records of Telban and Novak families. Our first stop was in the western part of Zagreb at a McDonald's Golden Arches operation for coffee to go. We saw many lovely Churches on the way to Novo Mesto. Our next stop was in downtown Novo Mesto about 44 miles from Zagreb under an umbrella of a "pub" where we stopped and tried to get oriented in the town.

We visited the Church above the town to search for records about our ancestors. Unfortunately, there was no one at the Church and further, we were told the records might be at the "older" Church on the hill overlooking the town. While the rest of the family was looking over this Church I decided to look inside a large building next to the Church hoping it might reveal some data secrets – I also needed to find a men's "toilet" quickly, HA! While in the structure, I talked to a young lady, Sonja I believe, about the building and the area of Novo Mesto. She reported the building had been used by the Church in time past but now was a music school and a museum dedicated to the poets of Slovenia. She could not offer any suggestions as to how I might find or review any records of my Telban and Novak ancestors. On the way up to the Old Church on the Hill we stopped at a cemetery hoping we might find some kin buried there. We discovered the cemetery was too new for our ancestors to be buried there.

We proceeded about 3-4 miles up the hill to the Old Church only to find it was closed and there were no humans on the property – at least, if there were any, they did not make their presence known to us. The Church of St. Urban was constructed in 1620 and was located on the hilltop with a beautiful view of the vineyard-covered hillsides and the valleys below. A very large tree on the front of the property had a hole in the base large enough for a person to enter – the hole was a result of a combination of rot and many small fires. In a glass cubicle on the back, or east end of the

CITY BOY

Church, there was a full-sized statue of St. Urban dressed in his clerical robes. The girls thought it was "lovely".

On the way back to town, we passed many well-maintained vineyards. We stopped at one that had caught our eye on the way up the hill - the date on the entrance archway was 1917. The adults sampled some of the wine while the children had sodas. We purchased three bottles of wine at this winery which had facilities to serve large catered affairs on a patio under a large grape arbor. Again, the view from the terrace and patio was beautiful. We stopped at another winery on the 40-mile trip to Ljubljana, the capitol of Slovenia.

In Ljubljana, we had lunch at the Restaurant called Gostilna Sestica. Then we went to a castle we had seen advertised along the way. The castle had been built in the early 1500's as evidenced by the date of 1533 on a well within the beautifully rebuilt structure. Mike and his family walked up about 163 steps within the tower to have an overview of the castle and countryside. Mike took some video of those of us on the ground and inside the Chapel within the castle. A tree just outside the castle had been removed recently. The size of the remaining stump indicated that a very large tree had once screened the front of the castle. We returned to Zagreb and the Sheraton for the night

FRIDAY, 29 JUNE 2001

After breakfast, we checked out of the Hotel and started south toward Seline and Zadar. We saw no evidence of the civil war that started in June 1991 until we arrived at the City of Karlovac about 25 miles south of Zagreb. Just as we arrived at the edge of town we saw a three-story residence that had been riddled with small arms fire, particularly at the third floor level, as though the Serbs might have seen someone looking out of the window. Just a little way further we saw a series of buildings which had been abandoned as a result of the small arms fire and the fire of larger weapons or incendiary grenades/mortars. The destruction seemed to be concentrated in one area of the city, although as we drove along in the countryside, we also saw electric transmission line structures that had been broken and the wires were still on the ground. We also saw what appeared to be 345 kV lines on structures very similar to those used by Texas Utilities Company. We could not tell whether these lines had replaced the smaller capacity lines after the war or were present during the war. The low-voltage distribution-line structures in service were rather unique - the wood poles looked as though they had been hand-hewn and tied together in an A-frame configuration. The hand-hewn feature I decided was a result of residents trying to get service back quickly after the enemy had torn them down.

As we drove along, we saw several large grills in which whole lambs were being grilled. As we left Karlovac and headed south there were an increasing number of signs advertising rooms to let such as SOBE - Zimmer – ROOMS.

We stopped somewhere south of Karlovac to rest and have some refreshment. After the stop, Jacob took the camera and photographed things along the side of the highway. We stopped again, south of Udbina, to view the long valleys along the right side of the road. A few miles further we stopped at a restaurant in what probably was in the village of Plitvice. The owner was a jolly man who spoke a little of several languages including a bit of English. His face and body shape looked very much like that of George Knezevich, my father's good friend and former resident of Seline. The food was wnderful.

Just a few miles further down the road we came upon a totally destroyed and abandoned structure that appeared to have been a restaurant and possibly a place with rooms to let. The structure had been fired on with small and large caliber shells and then burned out – obviously, it was a target for soldiers who wanted to destroy a target of no military value. I believe this was another example of the Serbs attempt to destroy the morale of the civilian population. We saw a man painting a complicated piece of graffiti on a wall observable from the highway. The design was not far enough along to know what the final message would be. Jacob discovered a snake while roaming over this property-he left the area very quickly. The view from this place of the Velebit Mountains in the sunlight was beautiful.

CITY BOY

Not too much farther down the road, we came upon a large bridge which had a 10-12 foot penstock on top which started up in the mountains to our right and connected to a structure in the valley below on the left side of the road. We also saw, what appeared to be, an abandoned plant alongside the large lake. This fact, along with the many large open pits in the area, made it look like an abandoned refinery of sorts. We found out later that an aluminum-ore reduction plant had been in operation there before the war. The penstock carried water pumped-up and stored in a mountain lake off-peak then released for the turbine-generators during the peak on the following day.

As we continued down the mountain headed west toward Seline, we got our first glimpse of an arm of the Adriatic Sea at a highway intersection in the village of Meslenica. Later in the week we headed south toward Zadar at this same intersection. We reached Seline wondering how we'd find the home of Milan and Mira Jurlina when Mike made a fast left turn at a Jurlina sign This was the home of Milan and Mira. What a memorable occasion for us all since this was the first visit to Seline of any descendants of my father who immigrated to the USA in mid-October of 1913. The Jurlina home is a three-story structure constructed over the last 20-years by Milan and his family during their vacations. Only the second floor was complete and ready for occupancy while the first floor was almost completed and the third floor is yet to be finished.

Joseph Jurlina

After greeting our hostess Mira Jurlina, the children and adults went out to view the sea and surrounding area. This year Mira preceded Milan to Seline by about three weeks to be ready for her visitors - he was to arrive about the middle of July. We were sorry to miss him. The shore opposite this home is very lightly developed in part I was told because of a high wind, called Bora, which originates in the mountains and blows toward the opposite shore. The Bora is a very fascinating thing to experience since, once it starts, it blows constantly, sometimes for more than a day at a time with wind velocities of from 10 to 50 miles per hour. The natives say it is much worse in the winter months.

Looking west-northwest along the coast we saw the ruins of an old castle on the end of the shore curving toward the north. This castle ruin, dating back to Roman times, reportedly settled quite a bit into the sea during an earthquake some centuries ago.

We returned to Mira's home and sat down for our first meal with Mira on their beautiful balcony overlooking the Adriatic as the sun was setting – a very beautiful sight to behold and equal to the best anywhere.

SATURDAY, 30 JUNE 2001

After breakfast, the entire Dallas crowd and Mira went to visit Ante "Bele" Jurlina, my first cousin and son of Sam, who now lives in the stone home his father and grandfather had built in 1914. The home is just a short distance east and north of Mira's home and up the mountainside a few hundred yards. Bele turned 70 this year and recently returned to Seline after having lived in Germany for about 25 years. He was a tinsmith or mechanic during that time and now has undertaken the job of remodeling the old homeplace. To date he has remodeled the kitchen with new appliances and a bathroom with modern fixtures. He had a triple heart by-pass about 3-4 years ago in Germany but is a vigorous and energetic man.

He met us at the gate of his property dressed in white shorts but barefooted as he expected the day to be a hot one. He showed us around the house and named the people in some photos he had hanging in his living room. One of the photos was of our grandfather Joseph Jurlina

CITY BOY

(1859 – 1939) taken when he was probably in his late 60's. Bele also had a picture of his mother and father, Sam and Barica, and his three brothers, Joseph, Tomas and Peter. His sister, not in photograph, was Lucija, who married Ljubomir Zuzu, and is the mother of Ljubica (Violet) Zuzu. Ljubica. Ljubica married Vinko Jarac and they now live in New York State with their two boys Jacob and Mark. Bele's older brother Joseph died in 1991 in Rijeke, while his brother Tom still lives in Belgrade. His brother Peter died in 1996. Tom is the brother who gave me all the data he had about the Jurlinas of Croatia. Of course, we had to partake of Bele's hospitality and drank some of his wine. On the patio we visited about all the family we could recall. There is an old smokehouse off the patio and in the smokehouse there is a large pair of leather high-topped shoes which Bele said he used while working in the garden. Fortunately, Bele spoke German so Jacob, having studied German at St. Mark's School in Dallas, translated our conversation.

Bele took us on a tour of the area around his home to see the large rock wall our grandfather Joseph had built, especially the large cornerstone. According to Bele the stone was so large that nobody could move the stone into place; however, one morning in 1928 after much discussion about the stone the night before, the family awoke and found that the stone had been moved into place. This confirmed all the stories we had heard about the strength and "know how" of our grandfather.

The Dallas crowd and Mira then went for a drive around Seline and stopped at Villa Antica, the hostel owned by Ante Jurlina, youngest son of my father's sister, Aunt Antica,. We assumed the building was unoccupied because it had been heavily damaged and left uninhabitable by the Serbian Army. While on the second floor we discovered that someone had been sleeping in a bedroom as there was clear evidence of ruffled bed linens and someone's personal belongings. We went back down to the first floor and were greeted by Frank Jurlina, the older brother of Ante, the owner of the building. In another moment or two a man, who turned out to be Ante, the owner made his appearance. Apparently, both men had been in the wine cellar of the structure and heard us walking about. We had a great time making introductions all about. Then Ante described how he and his brother, with help from others and some money from the Government, plan to rebuild the place for use as a hostel by 1 January 2002. After visiting the wine cellar, we adjourned to Frank's home that was immediately east of Villa Antica where we met Frank's wife, Bozica Banic Jurlina. Of course, we were offered wine to toast this significant occasion - a procedure we followed during each of our visits in relatives homes.

We then visited the Church where my father had served as acolyte when he was about 10-12 years old. All of my siblings and I had heard many stories about the Church and how our father had helped prepare the fire, and helped cook the meals for the priest. The Church is small and probably had pews for 40-50 worshipers. We then returned to Mira's home for lunch.

After lunch, Bele came to visit for a short time and then we all departed for the Seline Cemetery which was only a little more than one quarter of a mile from Mira's home. Most of the headstones had a Croatian phrase "TIHI DOM OBITELJ JURLINA" which, roughly translated, means "The quiet, or perhaps last quiet, home for the family Jurlina." We found data I had not seen before for Jurlina family members. I did not see a grave for Jacob, my great-great grandfather, who died after 1836.

On the way back to Mira's home, we visited Milan's parents home to introduce ourselves to Tome Jurlina and his wife Bozica - they live in a home just across the driveway from Milan and Mira's home. We had a wonderful visit even though none of the Dallas Jurlinas could speak Croatian. Of course, we had our very gracious hostess Mira to translate for us. We drank more wine during this visit - two hours and about one quart of wine later, we returned to Mira's home for our second-to-last night in Seline. Mira prepared octopus potato salad for dinner. It was one of the best dishes we had on our trip.

SUNDAY, 1 JULY 2001

After breakfast, we walked around the beach for a little while taking a last look at what had been our home for several days. There is a five-story house, at the left front of Milan and Mira's home, about 200 yards away that houses a restaurant on the first or basement floor. The building is painted white and is very prominent on the shoreline. When cooking takes place an exhaust fan on the kitchen-side of the place operates and sounds it like a buzz saw at high speed. I had been tempted to visit the place and suggest the fan be replaced; but my inability to speak Croatian kept me from complaining.

Bele invited the seven of us, six Texans and Mira, to his home for Sunday lunch. He had promised to grill some pork steaks for us so we were delighted to accept his invitation and arrived about 11:30 A.M. We were offered the customary wine or beer while we admired some old oak chairs and stools made by my grandfather Joseph. The furniture probably was at least 60 years old.

We admired the grape vines that were growing over the second floor banister and hung down to the first floor providing some shade to the area. We watched with great interest as Bele started the fire in his homemade grill and then washed the lettuce for our salad – obviously, he had done this type food preparation many times before. Pamela sliced the tomatoes taken from his garden and set the tables for lunch – some of us would eat with plates in our lap. Bele brought out a platter of pork steaks that looked like he had at least 20 pounds of meat prepared for grilling. When we questioned him about that amount he said that the men were to eat at least 2 kilograms (over 4 pounds) while the women would eat at least one kilogram (more than 2 pounds). We told him that if we complied he would have several sick people on his hands. As usual in an affair like this, the host ate nothing but kept his energy level up by drinking his beer as he cooked.

After our pork-repast, Bele took us all up the hill to visit the "old Jurlina homeplaces". It was on this last visit to the Jurlina compound that Bele proposed that Jacob should own the home where my father had lived in 1913 before he came to the United States of America aboard the U.S. Steamship Martha Washington. The stone house has not been lived-in for many years and will need serious repairs to the interior before it can be made livable. Billie took pictures of the houses and the goats housed in some of the buildings. After lunch we bid Bele goodbye and returned to Mira's home for a short rest.

Later in the day, we drove northeast up the coast a few miles to Starigrad-Paklenica to view some of the construction there and some ruins of buildings abandoned after the Serbian Army had been in the area in the 1991-1992 timeframe. On our return we stopped at the castle ruins that are visible from Mira's home. Only a part of one tower of the castle remains on a finger of land going into the sea. Based on the amount of grass and other crops growing around the castle, the land looked as though it was very productive. Mira opined "it was a shame that such productive land had not been put to better use by the people of the area". We returned to Mira's home in Seline so the children could take another swim in the Adriatic.

MONDAY, 2 JULY 2001

After breakfast, we drove up the coast about 4-5 miles to the Paklenica National Park in the Velebit Mountains to have a closer look at the Velebit Mountains. We parked at the gate and walked up the narrow paved road into the park in time to see several mountain climbers scaling the steep rocky-wall of the mountains. Some were up about 100 feet or more from the canyon floor while many on-lookers, such as we were, watched the climbing effort and technique. A little higher along the canyon road, we saw more climbers but this time on both sides of the canyon. On the right side, in a little wooded area by the creek, we saw a wheelchair and walkers parked by a tree and several climbers on the canyon wall. We did not know whether the climbers owned the equipment or the observers owned it. The wind in the canyon park was quite high and noisy – it may have been the reason the climbers did not venture more than 100-150 feet up the walls.

As we walked out of the park, we saw some beautiful cloud-formations, one of which, looked like a singer with his hand outstretched - I ventured that it was Jimmy Durante in one of his famous poses. We also saw the door to Marshall Tito's war-room deep in the mountain that reportedly could house and maintain a force of two hundred or more personnel.

On the way back to Seline we stopped at St. Peter's Church and cemetery at which Archeologists from Zagreb were making excavations around the property. The Church probably dates back to Roman times in the 9th or 10th Century. The digging there had produced some brass jewelry items which where bagged and tagged for display in the Zagreb Museums. I wondered about the propriety of the digging there but we made no comment. We made our final return to Seline to make pictures and pack our belongings in the van, then about 11 A.M. we headed south toward Zadar.

We drove around Zadar to view the seacoast and the many marinas with hundreds of boats tied up. It is a fairly large old coastal town and has many large residential areas. My cousin Ante had lived there with his wife and three children for many years. However, after the war started, the three children left and sought political asylum in England and Italy. Mira, the oldest, went to London very shortly after the Civil War started and is to our knowledge is still there today. Anita and Marin the younger children went to Italy as soon as they were graduated from school. They are there still – Anita married an Italian man and Marin is working there. On the way out of Zadar toward Zagreb we saw some buildings that had been damaged and abandoned during the war.

We stopped at a new and modern restaurant on the outskirts of Plitvice for a late lunch and had a bowl of the best goulash we had had since our arrival. The ice cream was good also, ha!

As we passed through the town of Slunj we saw and crossed the Korana River several times. On the north side of town the river bed dropped about 30 feet and we saw some very beautiful falls as the river had split as it passed around the town. A new observation deck was being built on the north side of town to give tourists a better view of the river and falls. In this same area we saw some transmission line structures (steel) which had been toppled by the Serbian Army during the war.

We arrived in Zagreb late but before sunset and had a bite to eat in the Fontana Dining Room - our waiter was Tomislav ---------. He told me his father had lived in Youngstown, Ohio where he worked in the steel mills there. I promised Tomislav I try to look up to see if he had any relatives still living in Youngstown and report to him what I found. I lost my notes with his surname and sent a message to the Manager of the Sheraton

Hotel - Tomislav was on vacation for a few days so we don't know if he got our message.

TUESDAY, 3 JULY 2001

The American tourists from Dallas had breakfast with Hrvoje and Nicholas Jurlina in the Fontana Dining Room of the Sheraton for a last goodbye (Dovidenje) before leaving for the airport. We checked in our Ford Transit Van and boarded our flight to Zurich, Switzerland. The return to Zurich was aboard the same British-made four-jet engine plane that was as cramped as could be with three narrow seats on either side of the aisle.

After a two-hour layover in Zurich we boarded a similar plane for Frankfurt, Germany and arrived there after dark. After a long walk through a maize of construction, we sought shelter in the Sheraton – Frankfurt Hotel where we had reservations, thanks to Pamela.. The hotel is located on the airport property..

WEDNESDAY, 4 JULY 2001

We boarded an afternoon flight on a Boeing 767 that arrived in Dallas in the A.M. of Wednesday, 4 July, 2001 early enough so that we could celebrate the National Holiday and fly our flag for several hours before sundown. We saw the movie "ANTITRUST" on the flight over to D/FW. We also napped a lot!

OUR TRIP TO NEW ZEALAND IN 2004 TO FIND MORE JURLINAS

We left home on 7 July 2004 headed for New Zealand via Los Angeles. We left LAX aboard a Boeing 747-4 and were aboard for about eleven hours before we reached Auckland. We picked up our Van and drove to the Holiday Inn Centra. We drove around for a bit and ended up at our motel to hit the sack.

CITY BOY

On Wednesday the 9th of July, about mid-afternoon, we did more sightseeing and then drove to the War Memorial Museum. It is a beautiful structure constructed about 1929 and has many interesting exhibits. Unfortunately, we were not in time to visit all the exhibits. A second visit is probably justified.

We then went downtown to visit the Sky Tower, one comparable to the Reunion Tower in Dallas except that this tower is much taller (about 1,000 feet tall). We had dinner at the base of the tower before boarding the elevator to the observation floor. The view of Auckland was worth the effort for the city is very nice, modern and clean looking.

The next day we arose rather early (at least the boys awakened early) found a grocery store to purchase groceries for breakfast. About mid-morning we drove to One Tree Hill to see the Obelisk and get a long view of Auckland. Of course, we all made photos of the sights. After this vantage point we drove to the marinas to see the boats there. We then drove through town to the Food Town Grocery to pick up some groceries for our dinner and breakfast. Mike, Pam and the children went to a Rugby game which started at 7:70 PM. Billie and I watched the game on the local TV and thoroughly enjoyed it.

After breakfast the next morning we set out for Kaitaia on the North end of the North Island and arrived at the home of Ivan and Mary Jurlina shortly after noon. Ivan is a descendant of Loui Jurlina who came to New Zealand just before 1900 from Zivogosce, Croatia to dig for Kauri tree gum. The gum was used to make varnish and covering for linoleum. We had lunch with all the Jurlinas numbering about 16 in Ivan's home. We visited with all the members and exchanged family information trying to establish our kinship.

After lunch our Michael and Ivan's son Michael arranged to find a motel in which we were to spend the next few nights. The children all arranged to see a movie in a local movie-house which turned out to be a small barn. Our children were cautioned not to speak too loud else they would be identified as "foreigners" and charged more for admittance. Later that evening as we were preparing for bed we received a telephone call from Ivan's son Michael who told us that **"the family"** had had a meeting and wanted us to come for dinner the next day and while there we could see David's home and dairy farm on which he milked 450 cows twice a day, and the home of Michael and Lisa Jurlina.

We spent the night at the Tampa Bay Resort not too far from Ivan's home. We drove to the "Ancient Kauri Kingdom Shop" in Kaitaia. This place was reputed to have crafts and furniture made in the area from Kauri trees for sale. The Kauri trees were buried in sand at varying debts for anywhere from 30,000 to 50,000 years ago by some gigantic event. The sap from these trees was considered a valuable resource for many years starting just before 1900 and lasted until after World War II when other chemicals displaced the gum from common usage. The Kauri wood has been found to be a very valuable source of beautiful wood. It was in this shop we saw a stump of a Kauri tree that measured about 20 feet in diameter. Inside the stump a stairway had been carved which was the access to the second floor of the shop. Tables, chairs and various pieces of furniture are made from this wood.

From the shop we went west a short distance to the Community of Sweetwater to find the family of Milan Jurlina, a descendant of Kleme Jurlina, brother of Loui, who came to New Zealand from Zivogosce, Croatia about 1900 to dig for gum of the Kauri tree. We contacted Victor, brother of Milan, by phone to find directions to his home - he said to start out toward Sweetwater and we would not have any problem. So, we started to Sweetwater and before we had gone very far we came upon a home on a slight hill and in the front yard was a half a tree log about three feet in diameter and 20 feet long with the name JURLINA engraved in the face of the log. It was there we met Victor Jurlina, brother Milan Jurlina and his wife Annette.

They were very eager to tell us the story about their Jurlina ancestors as the earliest Croatia gum diggers from the Dalmatian area on the south coast of Croatia. The local New Zealand citizens referred to these diggers as "DALLIES". Milan and Victor took us on a tour of their Sweetwater Museum just below their home on the hill. It was there that we saw all sizes of samples of Kauri Gum which their father had accumulated to display to strangers such as six Texans. Victor also took us to see the office their father, Kleme, had used for years before his death. It was also located just below the house on the hill and was a wooden structure about 12 by 14 feet. In it the Jurlinas had kept the office just as their father had used it with files hung from ceiling rather than in cabinets. Obviously, Clem (this was the spelling of Kleme he preferred when dealing with locals) had wanted his files to be "at hand" and within easy reach.

The next morning Victor took us on a tour of 90-mile Beach, a gum-digger's park and an Avocado farm not too far from the Jurlina Museum and Home. It was an interesting experience to see about 90 acres of Avocado trees loaded with fruit. We were told that the fruit was harvested just before it was to be shipped out to customers because it did not continue to ripen as long as it was on the tree. Victor had indicated he needed to be home at 1:00 PM to greet his sister Gladys, her husband Ron Oliver and other members of her family. Sure enough when we arrived back at the Milan home the family members had arrived. We were introduced to the family and then we left to go to the Ancient Kauri Kingdom Cafe for lunch.

After lunch we went back to Kaitaia to pick up Jacob's birthday cake. Pamela had managed to find a baker in town that made a cake in the shape of a large log, about 36 inches long and 5-6 inches in diameter, covered with chocolate frosting. We drove to Michael Jurlina's farm home which overlooked Ivan's property. Michael buys male calves from his brother David and fattens them for market. Michael then showed us his collection of Gum which he valued at about $30,000. The home and place were very nice and homey.

We then drove down the road a very short distance to David's dairy farm on which he has about 460 cows. David's farm is located on the other side of Ivan's farm. David and Nada's home is very new and very comfortable. We then went to the barn where the milking takes place and watched the procedure in process. We also visited the lot in which new female calves are fed. As we said previously all male calves are sold to Michael.

From David's home we drove back to Ivan's home for dinner. When we arrived we saw the large lamb being roasted on a rotating spit and sweet potato chunks being cooked in oil. In about an hour the lamb was ready

Joseph Jurlina

to serve. After dinner and compliments to Jacob, Ivan asked Jacob to try, in the future, to remember the place and circumstance when he celebrated his 17th birthday. There were 26 Jurlina family members present in addition to the six from Texas. This indeed was a very special occasion for all concerned because of the fellowship of the two Jurlina clans - one from New Zealand and the other from Texas. We were back at out motel by 10:00 PM.

The next morning was supposed to be a fishing trip for the entire Texas crowd; however, it was too windy to embark on the trip so we canceled and headed south for Rotorua, a holiday type town. It was raining, windy and cool so we stopped in Dargaville at dark. We found a motel and went on to dinner at "The Steak House" We awoke early the next AM and after breakfast we went on to Matakobid where we found a large Kauri Museum.

On the road south to Auckland we stopped at "The Coffee Hut" for lunch at a country crossroad.

We drove on to Kumeu and ran into Gladys and Ron Oliver. They guided us to the Kumeu Winery, started in 1944, and since 1992 operated by widow Melba Brajkovich and her two sons. Son Michael, six foot six inches tall, was there to give us a short tour of the winery. Gladys and Ron invited us to their home for supper just a short distance from the winery in the outskirts of town. We left them about 7 PM for Hamilton where we spent the night.

The next morning we started out for Rotorua and ended up at the "Triple One Five" Restaurant for lunch. After driving around for a while we stopped at the "Millenium Hotel". About 7PM we went to buffet dinner around the swimming pool. After dinner we were entertained by a native Maori dance group. After the scheduled program Michael Jurlina was invited to join in one dance and performed like a pro. I believe Michael enjoyed his participation as much as the rest of the family

Sunday we went to downtown Rotorua where we stopped to let the children do something fun and Michael along with Pam and the children did some wall-climbing for about three hours. All did great in climbing but

CITY BOY

I must admit that Sabrina seemed to have the most fun and enjoyed the challenge more than the others. We went on to Auckland to find adjoining rooms at the Holiday Inn Centre. At the airport we went to the Quantas Lounge for buffet and dessert where we met the children and their parents at the gate for 5:40 PM boarding.

The flight back to Dallas was uneventful but we were grateful for the safe arrival in Dallas.

To summarize the trip to and from New Zealand I would have to say we had a great and exciting time meeting the members of another limb of the Jurlina tree in New Zealand. I suspect that Jacob had the best and most memorable time because he celebrated his 17th birthday with Ivan Jurlina ands his family. We thank you Lord for another safe and enjoyable trip.

Joseph Jurlina

APPENDIX D: PEDIGREE

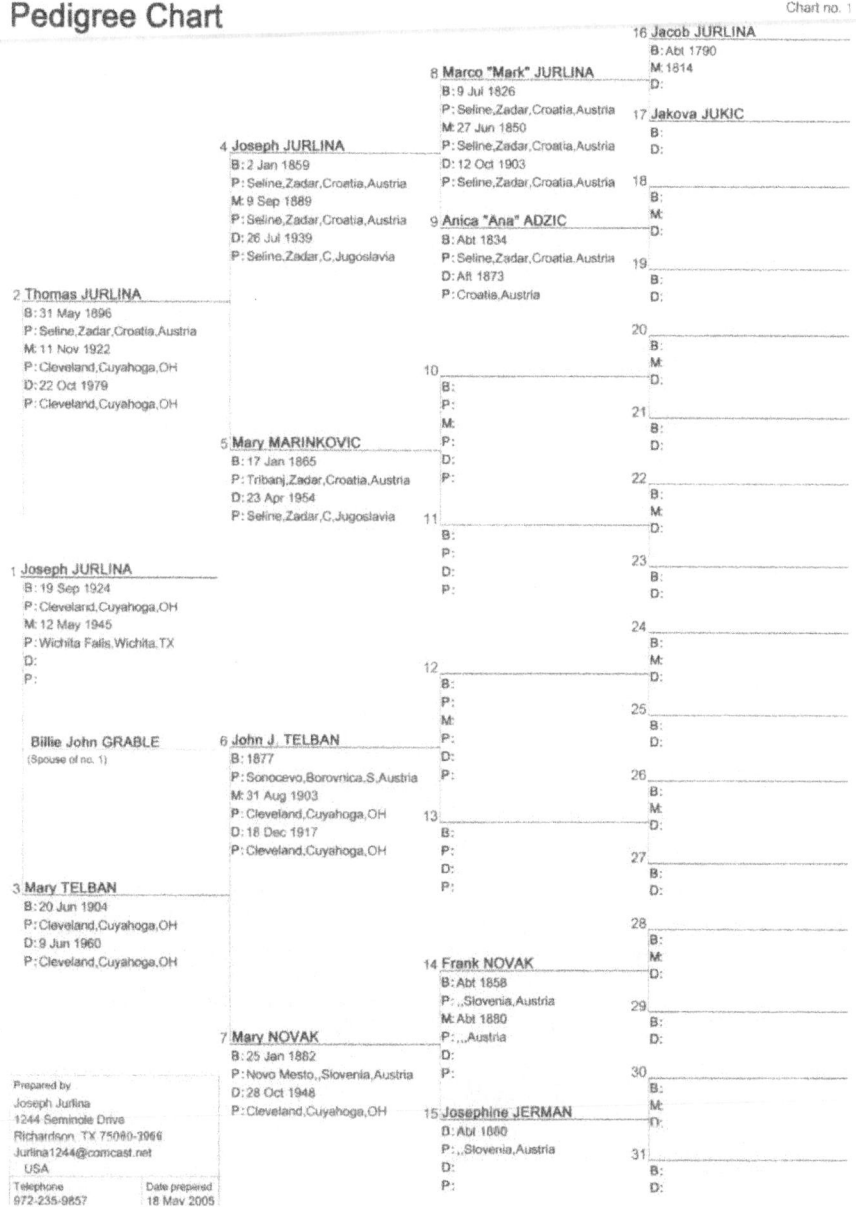

CITY BOY

```
MARY NOVAK = JOHN TELBAN   FRANK JERIC  FLORIAN VIRANT
                            └ "JULIE"                "SKEEZIE"
                              JULIA = CHARLES LASCO
                              JERIC  └ DAVID

MARY  = THOMAS JURLINA
TELBAN  ├ JOSEPH = BILLIE GRABLE
        │        └ CAROL ANN = WILLIAM KRUMM
        │                     ├ JASON KRUMM
        │                     └ KATHERINE KRUMM = RYAN CLARK
        │                                         ├ HOPE
        │                                         ├ ANASTASIA (ANYA)
        │                                         ├ JOSIAH
        │                                         └ JOSHUA
        ├ MICHAEL = PAMELA HASTY
        │          ├ JACOB JURLINA
        │          └ SABRINA JURLINA
        ├ EDWARD (DIED AGE 2)
        ├ THOMAS = LEONA MALNAR
        │         ├ LINDA = EDWARD BAZNIK
        │         │        ├ EDWARD
        │         │        ├ MICHAEL
        │         │        ├ STEPHEN
        │         │        └ EMILY
        │         ├ NANCY = GREG PROSSER
        │         │        ├ RYAN
        │         │        ├ ANNA
        │         │        └ ALAN
        │         └ THOMAS = MARY
        │                   ├ MARIELLE
        │                   └ PETER
        ├ ROBERT = ① DOROTHY THALER / ② ELLA
        └ MARY JANE = WILLIAM (BILL) ELAM
                     ├ KRISTIE = BRYAN HULSEY
                     ├ MICHAEL = TINA M
                     │          ├ GABRIELLE
                     │          └ OWEN       (girl)
                     └ JENNIFER

            ("ANNIE")  ①
ELIZABETH   ANNA     = WILLIAM AVENMARG / ② JOHN JASKO
            TELBAN    ├ ELSIE (AVENMARG) YECK = GORDON YECK
                      │                        ├ PATRICIA
                      │                        └ GORDON
                      ├ WILLIAM = BONNIE       └
                      │          └ BLAKE = JONI
                      └ RICHARD

            ("FANNIE")  ①
            FRANCES  = JOSEPH SIMONCIC / ② ELI RANTOVICH
            TELBAN    └ GENEVIEVE (SIMONCIC) = RICHARD LASKOWSKY / ② WARD
                                              ├ RICHARD
                                              ├ LYNN
                                              └ LAURA

            ("PEPPY")
            JOSEPHINE = FREDERICK (FRITZ) ZERULL
            TELBAN     ├ JOAN "JOANIE"
                       └ MARGARET "COOKIE" (MARGE)

            ("ANGIE")
            ANGELA   = WALTER PASTWA
            TELBAN

            ("JOHNNIE")
            JOHN     = THERESA MARICH
            TELBAN    ├ DOLORES (TELBAN) GIELNIK
                      ├ THERESA (TELBAN) SULLIVAN
                      ├ JOHN J. TELBAN JR
                      └ RONALD TELBAN
```

***For more genealogy information, visit www.Jurlina.com

Joseph Jurlina

LOVE YOU, GRANDY!
♥ *KATIE*

www.ingramcontent.com/pod-product-compliance
Lightning Source LLC
Chambersburg PA
CBHW051749040426
42446CB00007B/281